Business
Dashboards

Business Dashboards

A Visual Catalog for Design and Deployment

Nils Rasmussen

Claire Y. Chen

Manish Bansal

WILEY

John Wiley & Sons, Inc.

Published by John Wiley & Sons, Inc., Hoboken, New Jersey.

Published simultaneously in Canada.

For general information on our other products and services, or technical support, please contact our Customer Care Department within the United States at 800-762-2974, outside the United States at 317-572-3993 or fax 317-572-4002.

Wiley also publishes its books in a variety of electronic formats. Some content that appears in print may not be available in electronic books.

For more information about Wiley products, visit our Web site at http://www.wiley.com.

Library of Congress Cataloging-in-Publication Data:

Rasmussen, Nils, 1964-
    Business dashboards : a visual catalog for design and deployment / Nils H. Rasmussen, Claire Y. Chen, Manish Bansal.
        p.   cm.
    Includes index.
    ISBN 978-0-470-41347-0 (pbk.)
        1. Dashboards (Management information systems)   I. Chen, Claire Y., 1965-   II. Bansal, Manish, 1974-   III. Title.
    HD30.213.R37   2009
    658.4'038011—dc22
                                                                                2008042936

Printed in the United States of America

10 9 8 7 6 5 4 3 2 1

Contents

Preface

We now live in an information society, and more than ever managers are inundated with data. For managers to make the best possible decisions in the shortest amount of time, it is essential to turn data into structured information and then present this information to them in a format that is easy to read and that supports analysis. In recent years, software vendors have embraced this need, and now numerous solutions, commonly referred to as dashboards, have emerged on the market.

An effective deployment of dashboards within an organization can dramatically reduce the need for financial and operational reports. It will also support better decision making and ultimately help improve performance. Mid-sized and large companies typically have hundreds of different reports coming out of their accounting systems and their operational databases, and creating and maintaining such reports comes at a significant cost. In addition, because the consumers of the reports typically do not have the skills or the access right to the reporting tools used to create or modify report templates, they often end up exporting them to Microsoft Excel spreadsheets to make adjustments and to add graphics and formatting, among other things. This further adds to the cost and the pain involved in keeping reports up to date and validated.

Because most dashboard tools are highly graphical, dynamic, and easy to use, with simple training users across an organization can be empowered to monitor and analyze the information relevant to their areas of responsibility and to make informed decisions. Few dashboards survive in the long run unless they are based on the proper back-end infrastructure, such as a data warehouse and Online Analytical Cubes (OLAP) to keep the data up-to-date and correct. Because data architecture is so important for the long-term success of dashboards, it is covered in detail in this book.

Companies, educational institutions, and government organizations alike are starting to discover the power of dashboards to drive better performance, and this book discusses all the various activities and technologies you should know about before, during, and after a dashboard implementation. In particular, a deep focus is placed on real-life dashboard examples so that you quickly can find relevant ideas for your own project and help your own organization benefit from this powerful technology.

Book Summary

This book consists of four parts and appendices:

- Part 1: Introduction to Dashboards
- Part 2: Creating the Right Business Intelligence Architecture for Dashboards
- Part 3: Dashboard Design
- Part 4: Managing a Dashboard Project
- Appendices

Part 1, Introduction to Dashboards, introduces you to the world of dashboards. The discussion starts out by defining what most people expect a business dashboard to be and then covers the quickly rising popularity of this technology. There are multiple categories of dashboards, and each one is covered in brief. Also covered are the key activities you should be prepared to handle in order to get your organization ready for dashboard deployment. Finally, the last chapter in Part One takes you through the process of creating your key performance indicators (KPIs).

Part 2, Creating the Right Business Intelligence Architecture for Dashboards, takes a deep dive into the architecture needed to support long-lasting, high-impact dashboards. It explains why a good architecture is almost always essential to support business intelligence tools. This passage contains chapters covering both real-time and data warehouse–based dashboards. Part 2 then evolves into a description of the various technical deployment options. Finally, Key Performance Indicators (KPIs) and their relationship to data warehousing, performance, and dashboard deployments are discussed.

Part 3, Dashboard Design, provides a step-by-step process for dashboard design and contains a number of layout tips. Readers will also find a large number of real-life dashboards that offers ideas and concepts to support their own projects. Each dashboard has been categorized to make it easy to find; there is also a standard set of descriptors for each item to enable ranking and sorting to pick the ones that will be used as blueprints in a real-life implementation. Various examples of strategic, tactical, and operational dashboards are covered.

Part 4, Managing a Dashboard Project, goes into detail as to how an implementation project can be organized. Chapters discuss user motivation, project planning, and kick-off meetings and provide tips to keep a project on track. Examples of various project management tools are also provided.

At the end of the book, you will find five appendices. These cover software selection tips, installation, hardware recommendations, and security. The final appendix is perhaps the most important one, because it provides more than 1,000 examples of metrics and key performance indicators. These are organized by industry and major functional roles.

Business
Dashboards

PART 1

INTRODUCTION TO DASHBOARDS

The inspiration for this book stemmed from the surge in demand from companies and government organizations for dashboards that will empower their employees to optimize performance management. Our goal is to provide practical and high value-added content based on three underlying principles:

1. *The power of process.* It is much easier for a project team to go through an implementation when there is a structured process in place. Everywhere possible in this book, we provide step-by-step tools that can be used in a real-world implementation.

2. *The power of examples.* This book provides a large number of dashboard examples in order to give the project team and other managers as many ideas as possible for their own dashboard projects.

3. *The critical essence of good data architecture.* The authors propose that organizations need to deploy a solid and carefully planned data architecture to support sustainable and successful dashboards.

During customer engagements, we have experienced time and again that what can start out as a small project to implement a dashboard for one department within a company often causes a snowball effect and "I want a dashboard too" attitudes when other departments see the completed dashboard in action. Of course that means that along the way we proved to the information technology (IT) group that we could extract data from various source databases, and we proved to the end users that we could transform that data into useful metrics and present it in a user-friendly and attractive dashboard. Because both the data architecture and the dashboard's content and functionality are critical success factors to any implementation project, we cover each in detail in this book.

How should you read this book? If you are relatively new to the concept of dashboards and you do not have data extracted from source systems and ready to be used, we suggest you read this book from cover to cover. We have organized it so that it first informs you, then it provides real-world examples to give you ideas, and finally it guides you through the implementation project. If you already have a complete idea of the architecture, the desired dashboard(s) or how to run your project, then we suggest you go directly to the applicable parts of the book.

Exhibit P1.1 highlights the recommended workflow of a dashboard project along with related tools and advice found in this book.

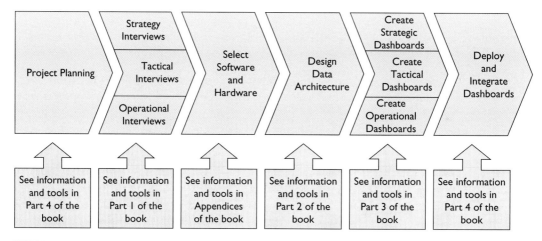

EXHIBIT P1.1 Dashboard Implementation Process

Dashboard Definition

1

I f you drive a car or fly an aircraft, vital information about speed, oil pressure, temperature, and so on is available to you through the dashboard in front of you. Gauges, red and green lights, and odometers are strategically positioned so that with a quick glance, without losing focus on where you are going, you know if everything is okay (or not) and can make decisions accordingly.

Just as drivers and pilots rely on their dashboards to do their jobs, managers today are increasingly turning to business dashboards to help them run their organizations. The ideas and benefits are very much the same as the example with the driver: Give managers a dashboard that on one well-designed screen shows the key information they need to monitor the items they are responsible for, and then they can quickly discover problems and take action to help improve the performance of their organizations.

Although this book is focused on the topic of business dashboards, it is good to have an understanding of the broader area of business intelligence (BI) software because they are closely related. BI software first arrived on the market in the late 1980s labeled as Executive Information Systems. They promised senior-level managers colorful, graphical screens with big buttons to make it easy for a nontechnical executive to see what was going on within the company. The major problem at that time was that data was not readily available because of proprietary databases (or simply no database at all) and lack of good extraction, transformation, and loading (ETL) tools to get data from the source and into the dashboard in an automated and meaningful way. It was not until the early 21st century that databases, ETL tools, and dashboard software had matured to a level that made sustainable, organization-wide dashboards a realistic possibility.

3

The term business intelligence was coined in 1989 by Howard Dresner, a research analyst at the Gartner Group. He popularized "business intelligence" as a broad term to describe a set of concepts and methods to improve business decision making by using fact-based support systems. Performance management is built on a foundation of BI but marries it to the planning and control cycle of the enterprise—with enterprise planning, consolidation, and modeling capabilities.

Since around 2005, BI software has been one of the fastest growing business software technologies in the world. As more and more users, vendors, and industry analysts have focused in on BI, a number of interchangeable or overlapping terms have been introduced. A more narrow area of BI is business performance management; the following definition emerged in 2003:

> Business performance management is a framework for organizing, automating and analyzing business methodologies, metrics, processes and systems that drive business performance.[1]

In other words, business performance management (BPM or Corporate performance management, Enterprise performance management, or Operational performance management) is a set of processes that helps organizations optimize their business performance. In this book we will mostly use the term Business Intelligence (BI) and we will categorize dashboarding as a part of BI. Most people agree that the area of BI includes the following processes and related technologies:

- Budgeting
- Forecasting
- Reporting
- Strategic planning
- Scorecarding
- Analysis
- Dashboarding
- Data mining
- Data warehousing

In summary, BI helps businesses make efficient use of their financial, human, material, and other resources. Good executives have always sought to drive strategy down and across their organizations, but without proper decision support systems they have struggled to transform strategies into actionable metrics. In addition, they have grappled with meaningful analysis to expose the cause-and-effect relationships that, if understood, could give valuable insight for their operational decision makers.

BI software and related methods allow a systematic, integrated approach that links enterprise strategy to core processes and activities. "Running by the numbers" now means something in the form of planning, budgeting, reporting, dashboarding, and analysis and can give the measurements that empower management decisions. When properly implemented, these systems and processes also motivate information workers to support organizational objectives by giving them actionable tools, objectives, and information.

Data warehouses and Online Analytical Processing (OLAP) (see Part 2 for more detail) are two of the fundamental technologies that have supported the adaptation and long-term success of modern dashboards. Whereas the data warehouse gathers, organizes, and stores information from various internal and external data sources, OLAP adds business logic to data by calculating and aggregating it. Together, these two technologies allow a dashboard to

- Display data that originally came from many sources
- Display metrics that are the result of simple or complex calculations
- Quickly provide new information on the screen, with minimal processing time
- Offer drill down from summary data to detailed transactions

For managers, dashboarding is now perhaps the most popular area of their BI strategy, and after about 20 years of evolution in BI software and related technologies, this business tool is coming of age.

Finally, just as there has been an evolution in the equipment available in a car's dashboard, there has been an evolution driving business dashboard technology. Whereas the first dashboards predominantly were a set of "cool" charts and indicators placed on a single screen or piece of paper, today's dashboards are increasingly more versatile (see Exhibit 1.1).

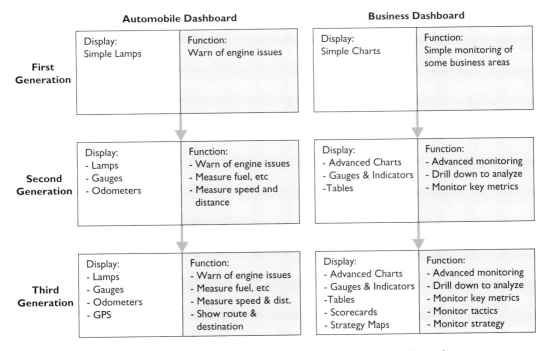

EXHIBIT 1.1 Evolution of Automobile Dashboards versus Business Dashboards

Automobile dashboards are now starting to include GPS (geographic positioning system) screens. Drivers not only know how fast they are going and how much gas is left; they can also plot the destination, select a route, and monitor the course on the GPS screen. Just like an organization's strategy and tactics, the GPS allows drivers to have a structured plan for where they are going and how they are getting there. Along the same lines, many of today's business dashboards can include strategy maps and scorecards, thereby integrating the monitoring of strategy and tactics along with the other analysis provided by the dashboard, so that at any point in time an information worker can stay on course.

This book is focused on how to successfully deploy dashboard technology with valuable metrics and graphical components to help your organization's employees manage and improve performance.

NOTE

1. David Blansfield, *Business Performance Management Magazine*, June, 2003.

Dashboards' Role in a Business Intelligence Solution

2

S ome dashboards may be used completely stand-alone, but more typically they are integrated with—or deployed as part of—a larger business intelligence (BI) solution that serves a number of other performance management functions (see Exhibit 2.1).

ENTERPRISE PORTALS

One of the most popular mass-deployment platforms for dashboards is an enterprise portal. Also known as an *enterprise information portal* (EIP) or *corporate portal*, an *enterprise portal* is a framework for integrating information, people, and processes across organizational boundaries.

When dashboards that support portals are deployed, the resulting solution provides several benefits to an organization:

- Users have a single location to access their dashboards as well as documents, presentations, and online discussions, along with other applications.
- Single sign-on is made possible (as opposed to maintaining multiple passwords and having to log in to multiple applications).
- Efficiency is increased as users can go to a single place to access a variety of related and unrelated information.
- A central point is established for an organization to deploy many or all of its BI applications.

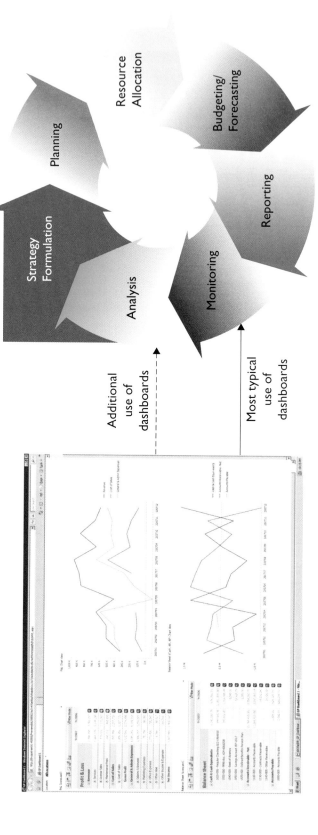

EXHIBIT 2.1 Dashboards and Performance Management

Not all BI applications support portal deployments, but all web-based applications can be accessed through hyperlinks, and as such the links can be embedded in the most relevant areas of a dashboard portal page. This can aid users in providing access to information that has relevant context to a dashboard or a component on a dashboard. For example, a hyperlink to a detailed financial report could be placed next to a financial chart showing actual and budget figures for an entire Profit and Loss report.

DASHBOARDS AND STRATEGY

Once an organization has developed strategies and tactics, it can use strategy maps and scorecards that help managers visualize and track their goals and tactics. Modern dashboards (often as part of deployments in portals) can then display or integrate with these tools. Well-planned and well-designed dashboards can effectively display key performance-related charts and indicators together with strategy maps and scorecards to help an organization focus their employees on the most important performance-related activities and drivers.

DASHBOARDS AND PLANNING

What do dashboards have to do with planning? The main role of a dashboard is to provide a means for managers to monitor, analyze, and sometimes annotate (e.g., explaining variances in an embedded scorecard), and there are several strong ties to planning and budgeting:

- Displaying, analyzing, and comparing historical figures with budgets, forecasts and targets
- Focused dashboards for deep analysis of budgets and forecasts (For example, this can be particularly effective when dashboards are fully integrated with planning tools, and organizations utilize a continuous planning methodology. Managers can then analyze trends and variances in a dashboard, almost immediately revise a forecast, and then see it updated back in the dashboard in near real time.)
- Monitoring and sharing of strategies across business units
- Monitoring of resource allocation figures whereby business units can propose investments of discretionary funds in various programs and projects.

DASHBOARDS AND REPORTING

Although it is not typical to use major portions of a dashboard to display detailed reports (then it would be more like a "report-board"), it can be highly effective to embed *links* to reports within a dashboard. This provides managers with detailed views of information that can support analysis done in embedded scorecards and charts. These reports also offer a professional format for printing or e-mail distribution.

In addition, most dashboards do not reflect real time—that is, they are based on data that on a periodic basis is loaded from transactional databases into a data warehouse and into Online Analytical Processing (OLAP) cubes. However, in some scenarios, usually in operational dashboards, managers need to see detailed real-time information in order to support the analysis they do using a dashboard, and then real-time reports that pull data directly from the source database can come in very handy if the data is only a click away from the dashboard.

DASHBOARDS AND ANALYTICS

Most modern dashboards offer a number of important analytical features. These are important to users to enable them to answer most questions right from the dashboard interface without having to log in to other software packages or modules to do further analysis. However, for a number of years, while vendors are working on developing the "ultimate dashboard" that can do sophisticated analysis right from within the same interface, most business intelligence companies will connect the user to a separate module for such tasks.

A majority of the comprehensive business intelligence suites on the market today offer dashboards that are tightly (or lightly) integrated with powerful analytics modules that offer various functions such as heat maps, drill down, statistical analysis, data mining, predictive analysis, and the like. Together with business dashboards these specialized analytics tools further empower managers and analysts to support performance management initiatives.

3

Why Dashboards Have Become so Popular

I f you have ever been in a position where you either have too many data sources (such as ten reports from five different people) or you have to find and analyze information in hard-to-read spreadsheets or lengthy report formats, you do not have to see many dashboards before you want one yourself. So in the early years of the 2000s with software prices coming down, new business intelligence (BI) technologies hitting the market, and data sources opening up, dashboarding suddenly became a mainstream word in corporations and governmental organizations worldwide.

DASHBOARD BENEFITS

Here is a list of some typical benefits of dashboards:

- Improved decision making and performance:
  - Ability to easily identify and correct negative trends
  - Ability to make better informed decisions based on collected BI
  - Ability to measure the organization's efficiencies and inefficiencies
  - Ability to perform improved analysis through visual presentation of performance measures
  - Ability to align strategies and organizational goals
- Employee efficiency gains:
  - Increased productivity

- Saving time by eliminating the need for multiple reports
- Reducing the need to create and maintain large numbers of static reports
- Low training requirements, and easy to learn

- Employee motivation:
  - Users can generate detailed reports showing new trends.
  - More time can be spent analyzing data and less time spent finding, compiling, and formatting data.
  - Well-designed dashboards are more interesting than most "old-fashioned" tabular reports.
  - Dashboards provide a means for sharing strategies, tactics, and operational data that empower employees to understand objectives and to make the right decisions.

Due to the quickly rising popularity of dashboards, software vendors are now eyeing the possibility that nearly all business users in an organization might end up with a dashboard showing charts and key metrics relevant to their responsibilities. At a speech in 2007 where he discussed Microsoft's BI strategy and tools, Steve Ballmer, CEO of Microsoft, used the term "BI to the masses," in describing how the cost of user licenses will be so low that almost any company can afford to provide BI tools (e.g., dashboards) to all the organization's decision makers at every level. In 2008, Google joined this race by offering free dashboards. What used to be expensive technology for a few senior executives in larger organizations has now become a commodity. Of course, dashboards can be virtually useless unless the underlying software architecture ensures that the right type of information is available at the right time. Data architecture and how it can support widespread and sustainable use of dashboards is covered in detail in Part 2.

Due to all the potential benefits, a successful and carefully architected dashboard strategy can have a profound and lasting impact on companies, educational institutions, not-for-profits, and governmental organizations everywhere. As managers are starting to realize this, they pay increasingly more attention to dashboarding as a central part of their BI strategy. However, as many companies that were early adopters of the technology have found out, there are several places a dashboard deployment also can go wrong. Here are some examples:

- Manual data entry of supporting data or lack of automated data refresh in the dashboard
- Lack of hierarchies and business rules to easily and correctly aggregate and calculate metrics

- Lack of useful metrics and drill down/drill across to support decision making (i.e., requiring multiple reporting tools to answer a question)
- Poor dashboard design that turns users off
- Difficult to use dashboard technology
- Difficult access (e.g., requirement of multiple logins—as opposed to a single sign-on whereby a user needs to be authenticated only once)
- Lack of executive sponsorship
- Lack of proper user training
- Poor performance (i.e., need for a user to wait half a minute or more for information to be retrieved and refreshed)

Parts 2 through 4 will discuss numerous ways to ensure that a dashboard implementation will have a real and lasting impact within an organization.

In the case of a company-wide deployment of dashboards, managers at all levels can use the technology to drive performance. For example, the positions shown in Exhibit 3.1 could be using the technology to monitor and analyze important metrics.

Examples of Position	Typical Dashboard Content
CEO	Key financial metrics Key operational metrics Key statistical metrics
COO	Key operational metrics
CFO	Key financial metrics
IT Manager	IT-related metrics Departmental scorecard
Sales Manager	Sales metrics Departmental scorecard
Help Desk Manager	Customer service metrics Departmental scorecard
Collection Manager	Receivables metrics
Plant Manager	Production metrics Efficiency metrics Quality-related metrics

EXHIBIT 3.1 Sample Dashboard Content by Position

IF IT CANNOT BE MEASURED, DO NOT BOTHER

One of the key ingredients of successful performance management in any organization is metrics, and a dashboard is a popular interface to provide those metrics to users. However, if a company launches a series of initiatives to support its strategy, they need to have tools in place to measure the success (or failure) of those initiatives. If not, the company's ability to adjust its initiatives as time goes by will depend on subjective opinions and best-guess estimates (see Exhibit 3.2).

So, with business intelligence technology reaching maturity, organizations now have better tools than ever to measure their performance. The flow of data from the gathering point to a manager's dashboard could look like this:

1. *Data collection point*—for example a cashier's scanner or software that measures user's clicks and movement on a website or a banner ad
2. *Transaction database*—stores all the detailed data collected
3. *Data warehouse*—transforms, organizes, and stores data from one or many transaction databases
4. *Online analytical processing (OLAP) cube*—aggregates data and calculates metrics

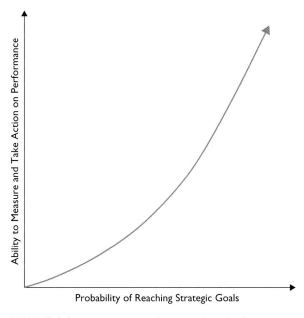

EXHIBIT 3.2 **Importance of Measuring Performance**

5. *Dashboard*—presents information to users and provides analytical features

With the proper tools and processes in place to measure performance and present the result to decision makers, companies, educational institutions and governmental organizations today are embracing dashboarding. As these processes and tools are optimized, improved performance will be the result.

Types of Dashboards

4

We have made this book as practical as possible, and when it comes to dashboards, it can be helpful to have a solid overview of the market before diving into an implementation project. Dashboard solutions now come with all kinds of content and with almost any type of graphics for all types of users. One of the main goals of this chapter is to provide key criteria to help you determine the right type of dashboard for each of your various decision makers.

This chapter discusses the various categories of dashboards. There are, of course, numerous ways people define and categorize dashboards. We have organized these into three principal types:

1. *Strategic dashboards*, which support organizational alignment with strategic goals

2. *Tactical dashboards*, which support the measuring of progress in key projects or initiatives

3. *Operational dashboards,* which support the monitoring of specific business activities

Before examining each category in more detail, let us consider how the three dashboard types relate to the people in the organization. A good way to do this is to extrapolate the dashboard categories on top of a chart that portrays each person's level of responsibility and their time devoted to analyzing data. Although it is not always true for all positions, it is likely that lower-level positions at the operational level of an organization with less overall responsibility have less time available for analysis. Senior executive–level

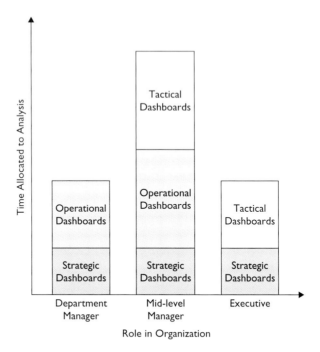

EXHIBIT 4.1 Managers' Use of the Three Dashboard Categories

positions at an organization spend more time on tactical issues but also have less time for detailed analysis. In between the two are the mid-level managers who are often involved with both tactical and operational issues. Many of them are assigned analysis and reporting tasks that encompass both areas, and that consumes a great deal of their time (see Exhibit 4.1).

STRATEGIC DASHBOARDS

By using strategic dashboards, an organization can monitor progress toward strategic objectives. An executive-level dashboard might reflect enterprise-wide strategic goals and corresponding key performance indicators (KPIs). Enterprise-wide strategic dashboards often "cascade" down to the department level, while retaining alignment to the corporate objectives. Working down from the global to the departmental level helps avoid creating isolated departmental dashboards. Strategic dashboards are typically highly summarized, highly graphical, less frequently updated, and include global, external, trend, and growth measures.

Strategic dashboards are often related to or based on the balanced score-card methodology of David Norton and Robert Kaplan,[1] which provides a method for determining and achieving organizational goals.

TACTICAL DASHBOARDS

Organizations use tactical dashboards to monitor progress and related trends for each of their strategic initiatives. This can include key projects, and both the initiatives and the projects are quite often measured against a preset goal (e.g., a budget or a target). Because tactical dashboards can be focused, they are ideally deployed with a technology that allows for drill down to detail and "slicing and dicing" the data—for example, to analyze why certain targets are not being met and where the problem is occurring.

As data warehouse and dashboard technologies become easier, faster, and cheaper to deploy, companies and governmental organizations can be expected to make increasing use of tactical dashboards to help internal and external stakeholders monitor progress on important initiatives.

OPERATIONAL DASHBOARDS

This category includes dashboards used to monitor business processes, business activities, and complex events. Usually, the display will provide daily or weekly updates or near real-time charts and reports that illustrate the status of business or manufacturing processes. Because managers use the dashboards frequently, they can discover issues and take action to fix problems or take advantage of opportunities. Because of the practical nature of operational dashboards, they are most typically used at the departmental level (where "operations take place") and not at the senior executive level. Senior executives would typically use a tactical or strategic dashboard to monitor just a point-in-time aggregate metric or two from each operational dashboard.

Similar to tactical dashboards, the narrow scope (sales, help desk services, etc.) of operational dashboards dictates more detailed information with strong analytical functionality to perform root-cause analysis on the displayed data.

Given limited space (sometimes referred to as real estate) available on a single dashboard screen, and, as discussed previously, the fact that managers at different levels in the organization are looking for dashboards tailored

	Dashboard Category		
Business Unit	**Strategic**	**Tactical**	**Operational**
Manufacturing	Reduce product return rate from 3% to 1%	– Implement a new quality control system by end of the year – Implement quality review meetings once a month with key suppliers	– Number of returns by product by month – Number of returns, Actual versus Target
Sales	10% increase over last year	– 20% increase in Product X sales in Europe over last year – Launch Product Y by September 1st	– Sales by department this month versus last month – Sales by sales person – Top 10 customers
Services	Reduce customer complaints to 2% less than Y% (industry benchmark)	Install new help desk software and train staff on it by October 1st	– Number of support calls year to date (YTD) versus last year YTD – Number of customer complaints per week and month
Human Resources	Increase employees retention rate to 90% by September 1st, this year	– Implement profit sharing plan by July 1st – Hire recruiter by October 1st, that can find the "right" employees	– Employee retention rate trend – Average employee satisfaction score
Finance	Reduce Average Outstanding Balances from 55 days (last year) to 45 days	– Hire two additional Collections persons	– Average Outstanding Balance by month this year – Top 5 customers with highest outstanding balance

EXHIBIT 4.2 Metrics by Business Unit and Dashboard Category, with Examples

to their responsibilities, it is clear that organizations that are serious about dashboarding will design layouts tailored to the needs of their target users. To help in planning for the types of dashboards users might request, we have created a chart with examples that shows a further breakdown of the three main categories and their related content into more detail (see Exhibit 4.2).

NOTE

1. Robert S. Kaplan and David P. Norton, *The Balanced Scorecard: Translating Strategy into Action,* (Harvard Business School Press, 1996).

Designing Metrics and Key Performance Indicators

5

The following sections will take you through a series of recommended steps to arrive at the metrics that are right for *your* organization. In the eagerness to get dashboard projects off the ground, managers frequently overlook the importance of proper definition and development of performance measures, and the result can be stranded projects or the need to redo data architectures and dashboards. Hence, the goal is to provide you with insight and practical ideas that you can use to help your management team develop strategic metrics and key performance indicators (KPIs) to drive the long-term success of your dashboards in a way that ultimately supports improved decision making and performance.

This chapter is undoubtedly the most important one in Part 1 of this book. Here information is provided to help you design the metrics that will be the very essence of your dashboards.

DIFFERENCE BETWEEN METRICS AND KPIS

Before you start coming up with metrics and KPIs in this part of your dashboard project, it is important that you and the entire team are clear on the difference between the two. This difference is illustrated in Exhibit 5.1.

In other words, a KPI is a metric, but a metric is not necessarily a KPI. A metric is really a measure of anything. A KPI, however, is meant to be a measure "that matters" and that ideally can be acted on. An organization has many metrics, but typically just a few KPIs. This is often the challenge when

EXHIBIT 5.1 Difference between Metrics and KPIs
Source: www.wikipedia.org

a management team meets to agree on a short list of key measures for use in its proposed dashboards and scorecards.

A KPI is a metric that is tied to a target measure. Typically, KPIs are represented as a ratio (percentage) of an actual figure compared to a predefined target figure. They are usually displayed as, or accompanied by, a graphical symbol such as a traffic light, to make it easy for users to instantly see whether they are on target or above or below the target.

In summary, well-designed KPIs help organizations spend more time on the important activities that drive performance and less time on activities that are not as relevant. Because KPIs generally are the most important of an organization's metrics, they are frequently the most valuable content of dashboards; therefore, most of this chapter focuses on KPI development.

TEN STEPS TO SUCCESSFUL KPI AND METRIC DESIGN

The following steps are recommended for you to use in planning for a KPI design project:

Step 1. Build the team.

Step 2. Clarify and agree to the organization's strategies and tactics.

Step 3. Decide on dashboard categories and prioritize.

Step 4. Choose organizational deployment.

Step 5. Create a list of KPIs and metrics for each strategic objective.

Step 6. Test KPIs against framework.

Step 7. Select top KPIs.

Step 8. Choose presentation method and interactivity for each KPI.

Step 9. Document decisions and get sign-off.

Step 10. Design architecture and dashboards based on document.

At this point, each step will be discussed in detail. *Note:* If you consider your dashboard project to be too small in scale and importance to set up a KPI team and to go through all these steps in detail, you should still be able to obtain some value from the workflow and some of the tips.

Step 1. Build the Team

The person who manages a dashboard project should ensure that the business management team is fully involved in the definition of the organization's KPIs. Depending on the category of dashboard sought (see step 3), the KPIs should be developed by a mixed team of operational managers drawn from each area of the organization as well as from the senior executive team.

Here are some tips for the KPI development team:

- *Do not hesitate to bring in qualified consultants.* Unless you have an internal manager with a good knowledge of KPI development, think about bringing in a consultant with expertise in KPI and metric design from dashboard and scorecard projects. Although this constitutes an additional cost, the long-term benefits can be well worth it.
- *Ensure that strategies and tactics are clear to the team.* All the participants in the KPI meetings should have a good and updated understanding of the organization's strategies and tactics. It is strongly beneficial to have at least one senior-level executive in these meetings to ensure that the KPI team is fully aligned with the overall goals of the organization.
- *Encourage a diverse and balanced team.* Successful (or not) selection and deployment of KPIs and metrics will have a long-term impact on the organization as a whole and it will also affect the employees. Furthermore, members of the project team may have parts of their compensation tied to the KPIs, so a balanced composition of team members will allow for the best possible results.

Step 2. Clarify and Agree to the Organization's Strategies and Tactics

Except for measures in certain operational dashboards that are used for monitoring detailed operational activities and therefore may not be directly tied to strategies and tactical activities, all KPIs and many metric measures somehow support strategic initiatives. All team members should know the organization's strategies and tactics and agree to these before any KPIs and metrics are designed, to ensure maximum alignment and productivity.

Step 3. Decide on Dashboard Categories and Prioritize

As discussed in Chapter 3, dashboards can be divided into three general categories: strategic, tactical, and operational. Of course, what defines a dashboard are the measures it contains. In addition, the mandate from the managers who proposed the dashboard project should in most cases indicate the type of measures that should be included. If not, this is the last chance to get agreement on the project's objectives before the work starts.

Decide which dashboard category is the most important, whether there will be several dashboards, and in which order they should be designed. It is recommended to build a high-visibility dashboard first to get "a quick win" (this could already have been decided in the overall dashboard project but now is the chance to align this with the KPI design team). A quick win will motivate participation and heighten interest in the overall dashboard project within the organization.

Step 4. Choose Organizational Deployment

Based on steps 2 and 3, decide whether the dashboard deployment should be at the departmental/divisional level or at the top, and whether there should be a plan to then continue rolling out dashboards horizontally across divisions or top-down. Typically, it makes sense to start with strategic and tactical dashboards from the top level in an organization and then cascade the KPIs down to lower-level business units. This will make it easier to tie the dashboards and the measures together. Usually, these dashboards will include scorecards with scorecard indicators. Quite often, however, it makes good sense to roll out operational dashboards horizontally across the organization. For example, you may start with a dashboard for the sales department, then go to the customer service department, then go to accounting, and so on. The order in which you deploy depends on chances for a quick win, expected return on investment (ROI), departmental interest, availability of data, and so forth.

Step 5. Create a List of KPIs and Metrics for Each Strategic Objective

This is the time to design the specific KPIs and metrics that should go into the dashboard(s) you selected in step 3 and that are aligned with the deployment you chose in step 4.

(*Note:* Appendix E contains a large number of industry and functional metrics to help you get started.)

Performance measures (Metrics/KPIs) can be organized into five categories:

1. *Inputs*—indicates the resources used
2. *Outputs*—specifies the work performed
3. *Efficiency*—monitors the output of an activity in relation to the resources used to produce the output
4. *Effectiveness*—tracks the quality of the work performed
5. *Outcomes*—describes the results for a broad goal that is supported by the preceding measures

In arriving at your choice of metrics, it is helpful to keep these five performance measure categories in mind to ensure that your dashboard(s) ends up with a focused or balanced set of metrics based on the audience the dashboard is being built for (see Exhibit 5.2).

The key drivers for identifying KPIs are:

■ Having a predefined business process
■ Having clear goals and performance requirements for the business processes
■ Having a quantitative and a qualitative measurement of the results and a comparison with set goals
■ Investigating variances and tweaking processes or resources to achieve short-term goals

Exhibit 5.3 shows an example of KPIs related to three different strategic objectives, and the second example (Exhibit 5.4) shows KPIs related to the tactics that support the three strategies.

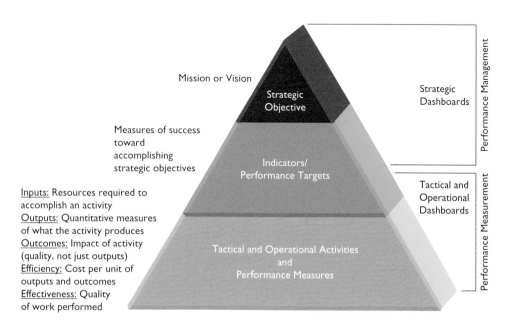

EXHIBIT 5.2 Performance Measurement and Dashboards

	Strategic Objective 1:	Strategic Objective 2:	Strategic Objective 3:
	Increase revenue by 10% over last year	Increase Net Profit by 15% over last year	Develop and launch Product X by October 1, this year
KPI:	Revenue increase (%), Current Year versus Last Year	Net Profit Increase (%), Year to Date (YTD) versus YTD Last Year	– Percentage completion of product – Percentage completion of launch activities

EXHIBIT 5.3 Example of KPIs in a Strategic Dashboard

Strategic Objective Supported:	Increase revenue by 10% over last year	Increase revenue by 10% over last year	Increase net profit by 15% over last year
Tactic:	Hold five additional lead-generation events every month this year over last year	Hire 20 new sales people by March 1st this year	Cut monthly telecom costs by 10% over last year
KPI:	(Number of monthly events this year) – (Number of monthly events last year)/ (Number of monthly events last year)	Percent of hiring plan completed versus target	Percent reduction in monthly telecom cost year to date (YTD) versus YTD last year

EXHIBIT 5.4 Example of KPIs in a Tactical Dashboard

When it comes to the process of creating each KPI or metric, you can use the following criteria:

- Business activity or initiative that needs to be measured
- Users that will take action based on the metric
- Data source required for metric calculation

- Metric calculation
- Metric target to measure against

Step 6. Test KPIs against Framework

Once the initial list of desired KPIs has been selected, further "testing" of the KPIs can be done to ensure that each one is as optimal as possible before final selection and deployment into dashboards. Exhibit 5.5 gives a suggested set of test questions. Use the column on the right to score (0 is lowest and 10 is highest) each item.

KPIs need to be "SMART" (Specific, Measurable, Achievable, Result-oriented, and Time-bound), and this is a good rule of thumb to go by when evaluating new KPIs to use in a dashboard.

Finally, you need to choose metrics that are actionable, and there should be an action plan in place. In other words, focus on KPIs that can be changed with specific actions. This way, when users see that the indicators on a dashboard indicate a problem, they can take action to correct that problem with the goal that down the road the indicator will show that everything is okay again.

Step 7. Select Top KPIs

Exhibit 5.5 showed an example of an organized approach for the KPI team to define and to score each KPI. Based on the total score for each KPI, you can then rank them and decide which ones to move forward with. At all times, the underlying goal should be to arrive at a set of metrics that can be used in the organization's dashboard(s) and to be sure that these metrics are those that best support managers' ability to monitor and analyze performance. You do not want too many KPIs; that will divert users' attention from the ones that are important. However, you do not want too few KPIs as that will leave users "in the dark" in certain areas.

Test Question	KPI 1	KPI 2	KPI 3	KPI 4
• Specific?	4	9	10	9
• Measurable?	8	10	7	8
• Achievable?	7	10	8	9
• Result-oriented or Relevant?	9	8	9	10
• Time-bound?	10	8	9	10
Total Score	38	45	43	46

EXHIBIT 5.5 Test Questions for KPIs

Step 8. Choose Presentation Method and Interactivity for Each KPI

Once you have the list of KPIs defined and you have selected the ones to use in the dashboards, the next step is to decide on the graphical features and interactivity that should represent each KPI. This is where you want to carefully analyze the right use of:

- Colors
- Charts and gauges
- Traffic lights, arrows, and other indicators
- Interactivity for drill down, annotations, actions (e.g., approvals)
- Alerts

You will find detailed information on this in Part 3, where specific design and layout are discussed and where you will find numerous dashboard examples to draw ideas from.

To make it easier for the project team to suggest the right visualization components to go with each KPI, we suggest that you create a "storyboard" on which you draw each KPI with its related graphics and tables. There are several alternatives to use in creating a storyboard:

- Draw it on a white board
- Draw it in PowerPoint or other available software
- Use professional storyboarding software

Step 9. Document Decisions and Get Sign-Off

Once the KPI team has completed all the preceding steps, you should document the team's conclusions and distribute that document to all the stakeholders in the project, including the internal sponsor and the dashboard project team. This will give everyone a chance to review the KPIs that were chosen and to see why these KPIs were selected over others that were suggested. Finally, make sure that all key stakeholders formally sign off on the document. This will help minimize internal politics later on once you start to deploy the dashboards.

Step 10. Design Architecture and Dashboards Based on Document

Once the KPI design team has completed the KPI document discussed in step 9 and stakeholders have signed off on it, the work with the data architecture and the dashboard design can start. You will find a lot of useful architecture design information in Part 2, and in Part 3 you will find examples and tips for the design of the dashboards themselves.

A CLOSING NOTE AND WHAT TO EXPECT IN THE FUTURE

A majority of organizations within an industry have metrics that are very similar to those used by comparable peers in the same industry. In governmental organizations, this is even more true than in the corporate world. This can make the process of finding and defining metrics a lot quicker and easier. In the years ahead we can expect to see research companies, publications, software vendors, associations, and other organizations gather and share KPIs and metrics within their industries. Of course, this is not necessarily limited to sharing KPIs and possible good dashboard designs. Ideally it provides a foundation for sharing some of the actual measures so that organizations can compare (i.e., benchmark) their metrics to those of a similar organization or an industry average. As this process moves forward, a lot of "best practices" material will be available across almost all industries, which again will help companies and governmental organizations create the best possible metrics and dashboards to drive performance improvement.

Dashboard Scenario: Use Case

6

I n this chapter, we will take you through a business case scenario to help you understand how you can use dashboards to monitor performance of your business, identify problem areas, and solve real business problems.

CASE OVERVIEW

Company Background:

- AW, Inc. (AW) designs and markets bicycles, frames, components, and accessories for mountain, road, and touring cycling.
- AW uses a performance management application for monitoring, analysis, and planning.

Scenario Description:

- AW conducts a mid-year business review whereby executives discover that one of the AW subsidiaries (Germany) is facing competitive pressures and has been losing market share for the past six months.
- This use case demonstrates how dashboards can integrate the power of business intelligence and present all necessary information in one place and most likely from a single interface (depending on the software application), allowing executives and managers to monitor, analyze, and plan a solution to the business problem.

- Issues prior to using a dashboard/business intelligence solution include:
  - Limited integration. It was hard to jump from application to application just to get information.
  - Misaligned information. When information was found, there was no way to tie it back to corporate efforts and objectives.
  - Slow and tedious process. Identifying issues quickly, performing root-cause analysis required costly information technology (IT) and analyst time.

SCENARIO WALKTHROUGH

In this case we assume that all executives and senior managers have access to all information, meaning all the dashboards and analytical tools. This access can certainly be restricted in almost every application, based on users' rights, and is governed by security control (more details on this can be found in Appendix D).

When executives and managers are reviewing the dashboards, one of the first dashboards senior executives at AW look at is the corporate dashboard. AW follows the balanced scorecard methodology; hence its dashboard is structured in that fashion. The green, yellow, and red traffic lights serve as first visual indicator for executives and managers.

A quick look at the corporate dashboard (see Exhibit 6.1) revealed that there were two metrics that are in red, eight in yellow, and thirteen in green. For discussion purposes, we will focus on one metric that is in red—one of the financial metrics, the contribution margin.

Everyone at AW is now curious to understand why the contribution margin is below the plan. Clicking on the contribution margin row takes AW executives to another linked dashboard. This linked dashboard provides details of contribution margin by region, and it quickly shows that "Germany" is below plan whereas the other regions are ahead of plan (see Exhibit 6.2).

Now knowing that the problem related to contribution margin is a regional issue that relates specifically to Germany, AW executives then go to the sales dashboard (from the same application interface) to understand the sales trend. The sales dashboard presents sales over time broken by revenue, cost, and gross margin percentage (see Exhibit 6.3).

AW wanted to look at revenue and gross margin for all product lines by region. With two clicks on the dashboard, AW is now able to look at revenue and gross margin percentage for all product lines and across regions: Europe, North America, South America, and the Pacific (see Exhibit 6.4).

Although the process will continue to go deeper in obtaining more details for German sales, your attention is directed to a few things shown in the dashboard in Exhibit 6.4. You can see sales trend in the graph over time indicating

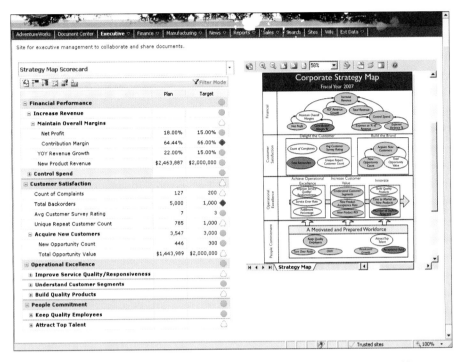

EXHIBIT 6.1 Corporate Dashboard Showing Key Metrics and Strategy Map

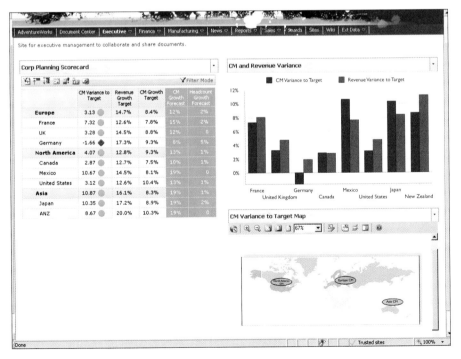

EXHIBIT 6.2 Corporate Planning Dashboard Linked to the High-Level Strategic Dashboard

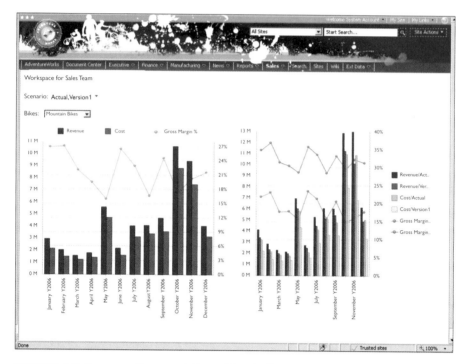

EXHIBIT 6.3 Revenue, Cost, and Gross Margin Percentage for a Product Line (Mountain Bikes) over Time

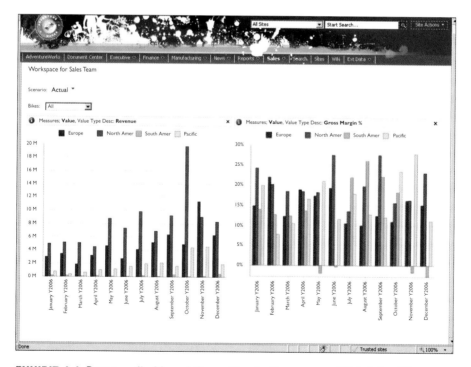

EXHIBIT 6.4 Revenue (Left) and Gross Margin Percentage (Right) for All Product Lines over Time by Region

that sales are best across regions mostly in the summers and winters—one could quickly relate this to the type of product involved, bikes—that would contribute to such a sales trend. You can also see that North America is the biggest contributor of revenue, followed by Europe, the Pacific, and South America; one could infer from this chart that AW has a strong presence in North America as compared to South America. This shows how dashboards can present a variety of information in one place allowing you to analyze the information in the direction you want and to slice and dice the data that is most relevant for the scenario or business area.

In this case, we will continue to drill deeper to see the gross margin for the European region only. Germany seems to have a negative gross margin (see Exhibit 6.5). With another click, executives are able to drill deeper into Germany to see that Bonn has negative gross margin through most of the year (see Exhibit 6.6).

Drilling deeper for Bonn reveals that the gross margin is negative for accessories and quite positive for bikes throughout the year (see Exhibit 6.7).

Drilling deeper into accessories reveals that one of the accessory items, Hydration Packs, is contributing to this negative gross margin (see Exhibit 6.8).

The executive team concludes that one of the items that has contributed to negative gross margin for Germany is related to the sales of Hydration Packs. The executive team sends a note via the dashboard application to the German country manager to find more details behind this (see Exhibit 6.9).

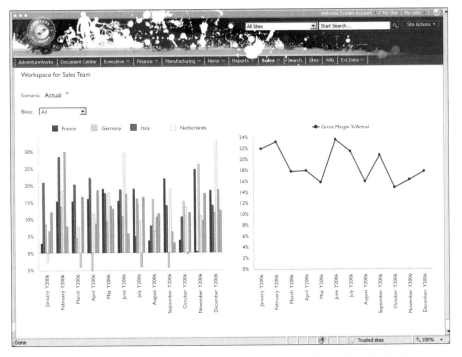

EXHIBIT 6.5 Within Europe, Germany Has a Negative Gross Margin (Left)

EXHIBIT 6.6 Within Germany, Bonn Has Negative Gross Margin Through Most of the Year

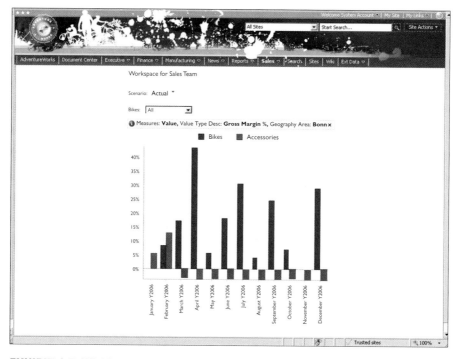

EXHIBIT 6.7 Within Bonn, Drilling for Product Reveals that Accessories Are Primarily Attributing to Negative Gross Margin

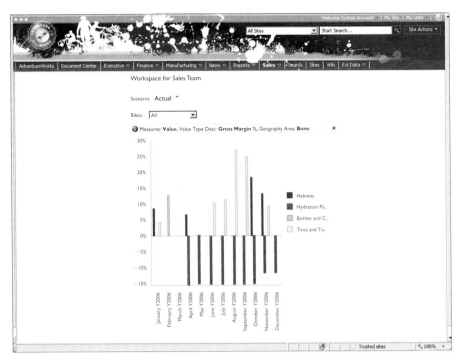

EXHIBIT 6.8 **Within Accessories, Hydration Packs Has Negative Contribution Margin Through Most of the Year**

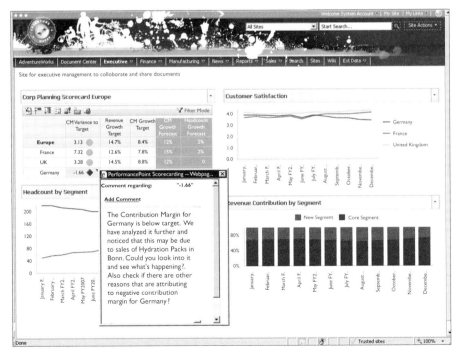

EXHIBIT 6.9 **Executive Team Communicates with Germany Country Manager via Corporate Planning Dashboard**

The country manager goes into further details and finds out that there were recalls for Hydration Packs in Germany, specifically for the packs manufactured by one of their local vendors, ABC Company.

The executive team moves forward to find other reasons that may have contributed to a negative contribution margin from Germany and a special task force team is put in place in Germany. Team comes back with the finding that the production line at ABC Company has a defective machine that has caused the problem that went unnoticed by Hydration Packs' quality control department. This analysis helped AW to control the quality of Hydration Packs and get the gross margins back to the positive numbers.

In this chapter, you have seen just one of the several ways an interactive dashboard can help companies find the root causes of a variety of problems that may be hidden underneath the high-level numbers for KPIs or metrics.

Getting Ready for the Implementation

7

The discussion up to this point has covered when and how dashboards have come about along with the reasons for their rapidly growing popularity. Chapter 4 looked at the three major categories of dashboards that organizations deploy and Chapter 5 covered KPI and metric design. So, at this point you may have started to formulate an opinion about whether or not your organization is ready to take advantage of dashboarding and which categories of dashboards will be best to start out with.

Whether the implementation is done by an internal team, external consultants, or a combination of the two, it will save time, money, and potential frustration if you are well prepared before the actual implementation project starts.

This chapter discusses the items you should have prepared before the implementation team rolls in.

PEOPLE-RELATED ITEMS

The following items are related to the people on the implementation team and the future users of the dashboards:

- *Who will be the primary users of each dashboard?* By clearly identifying the key users and documenting their information requirements and expectations from the completed dashboards, you can make sure early on that design and architecture decisions take these needs into account.

- *Who is the executive sponsor(s)?* There is usually a lot of excitement in any organization that announces a dashboard project. However, when the going gets tough, additional funding is required, team members need to be replaced, and so on, it can be critical to have a high-level executive that can be pulled in for key decision making.
- *Who will be on the implementation team?* Depending on the size and complexity of the dashboard project, there can be anything from a single person to a handful or more people on the implementation team. Typical roles include Project Manager, Business Analyst, Integration Consultant, and Data Warehouse Consultant. These roles should also be established in advance of the project. (For more details on this, see Part 4.)
- *Who is responsible for coming up with metrics and KPIs?* If you are implementing balanced scorecard as part of the dashboard process, this requires a well-defined set of cascading scorecards to which key performance indicators (KPIs) are related. Detailed KPIs eventually roll up into KPIs at the executive scorecard level. It can be a lengthy process to define all these KPIs, and oftentimes organizations rely on specially trained consultants to prepare all the KPIs on paper so they can be handed off in a formal document to the software implementation team. (For more details on this, see Chapter 5.)

TECHNICAL ITEMS

The following items are related to the underlying technology for the dashboards and the supporting tools and platforms:

- *What categories of dashboards do your users need?* Using the definitions provided throughout Part 1, establish the dashboard categories that will be included in the project.
- *What are the main components and metrics in each dashboard?* Based on the desired metrics/KPIs and dashboard category that will be designed as well as the reports/scorecards and charts that will be used to represent the information, use a white board, PowerPoint, or any type of storyboarding software to create a visual dummy version of the dashboard. This is highly recommended to do at the very beginning of a project to help all stakeholders visualize the end-result. (See Part 3 for in-depth information about dashboards and components.)
- *Do you have a particular color and layout scheme desired for the dashboards?* Organizations and individuals all have their own ideas and preferences about what is considered professional, attractive, cool, and so on when it comes to layout. Later in this book you are provided with some ideas and best practices to help you plan this part of the dashboard project. (For more details on this see Chapter 14.)

■ *Which data sources will be feeding each dashboard and related compo-nents?* Setting up integrations to your data sources and delivering metrics to dashboards is often 80% of the work in a project. Usually this includes the design of a data warehouse and/or online analytical processing (OLAP) cubes to organize, aggregate, and store the data. Because of the importance of this part of the project, you want to establish the required data sources at a very early stage in the project. (For more details on this see Part 2 and Part 4.)

■ *How often does each dashboard need to be updated?* For some organiza-tions, dashboards need to contain real-time data, whereas other dash-boards can be refreshed nightly, weekly, or sometimes even monthly. Regardless, you want to establish data refresh rates before you acquire the software and related hardware, even when the required features, speed, and so forth must be validated against your requirements. (For more details on this, see Part 2.)

■ *Is the funding in place (software, hardware, consulting)?* Do not start a project unless you have secured the funding. It will be disruptive and demoralizing for the project team as well as the future users to see a project stopped or delayed because of lack of funding.

■ *What software and hardware are needed and when do they need to be in place?* This includes dashboard software, extraction, transformation and loading (ETL) software, portal software, operating system, web server software, and so on. Based on the kickoff date for your proj-ect, these items should be in place well in advance. Also, determine whether a test environment is needed or if the implementation period will take place in a "live" environment.

■ *Are there any special features or platform requirements your users or infor-mation technology (IT) staff must have ("show stoppers")?* Rarely does a software purchase process include a due diligence process that encom-passes all current and future requirements. There are almost always features that are forgotten or compromises that have to be made. A structured and well-executed selection process can eliminate any sur-prises or "showstoppers" along the way. (For more details on vendor selection, see Appendix A; for platform information, see Part 2.)

PART 1 SUMMARY AND READINESS CHECKLIST

In this part we provided an overview of dashboards and the reason for the rising popularity of the technology. We then discussed the role of dashboards within the overall area of business intelligence software. We described the three different types of dashboards (strategic, tactical and operational) and how they are being used. In Chapter 5, we offered a detailed description of KPIs and how to pick the best possible metrics for the organization. Then, in Chapter 6, we presented an example of how an organization can apply dashboards to discover and analyze a potential problem. In the final chapter of Part 1, you got some tips to get ready for the implementation itself.

The goal of Part 1 has been to give you a good, general grasp of dashboards and related concepts before you proceed with the other parts of the book, which will go into more detail on the underlying architecture, examples, project management, and more.

The checklist that follows summarizes some of the key topics you have read about in the chapters in this Part and lets you score your skills.

Scoring: Not Sure = 1 point, Basic understanding = 2 points, Clear understanding = 3 points

	Score
☐ Target users for the dashboard	
☐ Difference between metrics and key performance indicators (KPIs)	
☐ Design tips for metrics and KPIs	
☐ "SMART" KPIs	
☐ Role of dashboards in a business intelligence suite	
☐ Examples of dashboard benefits	
☐ The three dashboard categories	
☐ Required software	
☐ Selecting the implementation team	
☐ Origin of dashboards	
Total Score	

Place your total score in the right box in the following Scorecard:

Status	Points	Color	Your Score
Ready	21–30		
In Progress	15–20		
Not Ready	0–15		

PART 2

CREATING THE RIGHT BUSINESS INTELLIGENCE ARCHITECTURE FOR DASHBOARDS

While there are many ways to build dashboards, all dashboards share the same purpose—that is, to deliver right information to people quickly so they can make right decisions. To do so, companies have developed various techniques and architecture to assist the delivery of the right content at the right time. In this part of the book, we will look at the various architecture and delivery methods that improve people's experience in using dashboards.

Why a Good Architecture Is Important

8

Many people implement business intelligence (BI) and data warehouse projects with great expectations. Minimally, they expect the projects to reduce the time and effort invested in their operations, or more ambitiously, they expect the projects to show new discoveries that can bring their companies to the next level of success. In one way or another, they want to see returns on their investments. However, many BI and data warehouse (DW) projects failed to deliver expected return on investment (ROI). While some of these instances have to do with failure in managing the expectations, many of these project failures also have to do with lack of expertise in implementing proper architecture for desired dashboards.

In 2003, and again in 2005, Gartner predicted that 50% of data warehouse projects would have limited acceptance or be outright failures. There are many factors contributing to such a prediction. Dr. Sid Adelman also said

> The average data warehouse takes three years to build and costs $3–5 million—yet many data warehouse project managers are thrown into the position with no clear idea of their roles, authority, or even objectives. It's no wonder that 85% of all data warehouse projects fall short of their objectives, and 40% fail completely.[1]"

Why do these data warehouse projects fail? Failures are related in large part to human errors (e.g., lack of resources, lack of sponsorship, inadequate project planning and management, inadequate user involvement, etc.), and some of the failures result from building BI on a flat-out wrong platform.

Frequently, a dashboard is designed by a group of business users who have a vision of what will help them to drive their businesses. By the time the project vision is turned over to information technology (IT) or BI consultants, it has become a data-crunching project. Many IT consultants focus on data mapping and scripting just to bring data out of a proprietary system. They have very little understanding of the implication of the end product. So, often the dashboards contain information that is irrelevant, the navigation of the dashboard conflicts with the purpose of the dashboard, or the performance is so poor that it blinds people to its benefits.

Having a purposeless or poorly performing dashboard is more common than not. This happens when the underlying architecture is not designed properly to support the needs of dashboard interaction. There is an obvious disconnect between the design of the data warehouse and the design of the dashboards. The people who design the data warehouse do not know what the dashboard will do; and the people who design the dashboards do not know how the data warehouse was designed, resulting in a lack of cohesion between the two. A similar disconnect can also exist between the dashboard designer and the business analyst, resulting in a dashboard that may look beautiful and dazzling but brings very little business value.

However, you may have a great dashboard with wonderful graphical displays and all the intuitive interactions. When you are viewing and navigating within the dashboard, you keep discovering new growth or pitfalls within your organization that you were never aware of before. As you spend time uncovering the performance of your organization, you are totally unaware of the underlying technical makeup. As time goes on, you start to rely on these dashboards. Ideally, you spend a few minutes every day to monitor your KPIs and analyze the causes to find business problems and the culprits. Then, you quickly go on with your business (e.g., drum up some more sales, bring the business issue to the attention of whoever can rectify the situation, revise the threshold to your next set of KPIs, or simply go out to play some golf). This is what a successful BI dashboard should be. "Business Intelligence," by its very own definition, is supposed to "be intelligent" and "enhance intelligence". It is a process that should bring insights (intelligence) to business users. Ideally, a good BI dashboard should help you find information at "the speed of thought," and the information displayed in front of you should quickly *tell* you what you should *act* upon. It is absolutely critical to have a dashboard that not only contains rich and goal-specific information but delivers it to you with great performance.

So, what can we do to make that happen? Obviously, it would require a solid yet flexible foundation. As a demonstration, we will give a high-level overview of various data warehouse techniques in the following chapters.

NOTE

1. Sid Adelman, *Data Warehouse Project Management with CD ROM,* Addison-Wesley Information Technology (2000).

Data Warehouse Techniques

9

W hen an organization acquires a database system, initially the focus is on how to get data into it. Of course, this type of data entry systems would store data immediately into the database. Frequently, the data entry system is web based and can save the data into the database immediately. This is referred to as online transaction processing (OLTP), the processing of transactions by computers in real time.

Very soon, people want to see what they just put into the database, as soon as they entered it. So, they start to build reports directly from this OLTP system. Most of the reports are fixed reports (e.g., "print me the name of the employee I just hired yesterday" or "what's the address for the customer 'ABC Co.'"). Architecture wise, there is no need for an additional server or additional systems, because the queries are very similar to the data entry form. Whatever was structured for data entry is identical to the query.

As time goes on, more and more people ask different questions. Human resources managers want to know how many people were hired last year and how much salary was allocated for high-grade versus mid-grade versus low-grade employees. They also need to maintain the organizational structure (who manages whom), employees' hire dates, the tenure, the raises, the benefit plan, the education and training plans, and so on, all on a much larger scale. Some of this information relates to other departments. For example, the salary relates to the payroll department, which calculates the withholding tax and corporate tax; the payroll expenses relate to the cash management department, which prepares funding for payroll. Corporate accounting has to take the payroll expenses into account when forecasting for budgets or cash flow, and each department or division manager has to take into account the cost of his or her department or division staffs, and so on. However, among all these managers and analysts, very few need to know the specific details of each employee (see business inquiries in Exhibit 9.1). For example, the payroll managers just need to know the employee's name, salary, and withholding exemption; they do not need to know the benefit plans. The cash management department needs to know the total payroll-related expenses as a sum for the pay period without any details; the department or division managers would mark up the salary of their members by a certain percentage to cover for benefits and corporate tax for their forecasting and budgeting; the corporate accountant needs to know the grand total of all the departmental forecasts which already includes the payroll expenses. Again, practically none of these managers care to see the employees' Social Security number or marital status, and certainly do not care to see employees' addresses. Very quickly, a small amount of data is relevant to multiple groups of people, all from different perspectives, which involve different calculations for different purposes.

From the system standpoint, the OLTP system is intended for data entry. The system performance is tuned to process a "single transaction at a time." It is neither prepared nor intended to perform calculations on a large set of data. As people ask different questions from different perspectives, these queries start to fight against the transactional systems to consume the limited resources. Pretty soon, the system slows down, and the data entry system no longer offers the real-time processing as it should. Meanwhile, the system

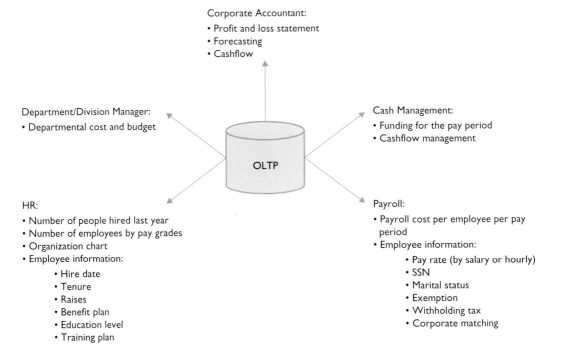

EXHIBIT 9.1 Business Inquiries from OLTP

also takes a long time to process the query results because of the ineffective indexing. Nobody is happy.

So, in order to offer data with enough flexibility, we would need a platform not only to share information but to deliver the right information to the right people quickly. Hence, some companies start their "data warehouse" projects.

DATA WAREHOUSE

A data warehouse is a repository of an organization's electronically stored data. Data warehouses are designed to facilitate reporting and analysis.

—BILL INMON[1]

When data storage is designed for the purpose of offering the reporting and analytic flexibility, it usually would involve some data retrieval and analysis, and some degree of transformation. Additionally, a carefully managed data dictionary would be needed as a critical part. Thus, the term Data Warehouse has been extended to incorporate management tools for extract, transform, and load data, as well as for managing metadata collected from source systems.

To design a proper architecture to support your dashboards, you would need to

- Understand different types of data warehouse structure and the purpose of each.
- Understand different ways of data replication and delivery methods.
- Understand the best query language for these data structures as to improve dashboard performance.

ODS

The quickest way for information technology (IT) to combat the performance issue in an OLTP system is to copy the data to another system. This way, one system can be used for data entry, and the other can be used for reporting. Such replication may be scheduled in various frequencies (i.e., daily, hourly, or every minute). Sometimes, companies would take advantage of their High-Availability System which is already set up for real-time replications for this purpose. Since we are copying data from one system to another, we may also combine data from multiple sources. In the process, we may also want to cleanse the data, so we can build a meaningful report on this combined data set. This is the birth of operational data store (ODS). We could say that implementing ODS is the first step toward building a data warehouse.

An operational data store (or "ODS") is a subject-oriented, integrated, volatile, current-valued, detailed-only collection of data in support of an organization's need for up-to-the-second, operational, integrated, collective information.

—Bill Inmon[2]

An ODS is intended to bring together multiple sources to make analysis and reporting easier. Due to this integration nature, creating an ODS sometimes involves some degree of data cleansing process to improve data integrity. In addition, an ODS is highly transactional, because it captures source transactions in "real-time" or "near real-time" fashion and often follows the same indexing as the source systems. However, some customized ODS' would model after dimensional structure instead of the transactional structure. This is to conform to data warehouse structure and loaded into data warehouse easier. In these cases, the ODS indexes would not follow the source systems' indexes. See the architecture graph indicating the position of ODS versus data warehouse and data marts in Exhibit 9.2[3].

The benefits of ODS include:

- Creating a separate environment to off-load the resources on the production OLTP system
- Creating a staging environment to "integrate" multiple sources
- Creating a staging environment to "transform" data for the data warehouse
- Providing a staging platform for the data warehouse

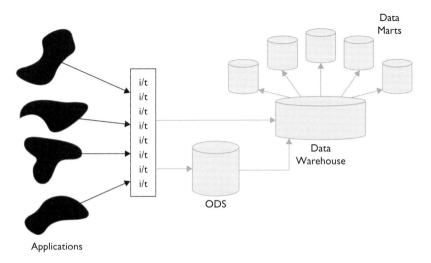

EXHIBIT 9.2 Architectural Positioning of the ODS
Source: http://www.dmreview.com/issues/19980701/469-1.html

Although some ODSs are not the exact replication of OLTP (i.e., it may contain cleansed data or restructured schema, etc.), ODS is still highly transactional. There is very little aggregation at this stage of process. The indexes are also designed for transactional reporting. Thus the types of reports or dashboards offered from ODS would usually have more detailed "listing" reports that are within shorter time range with some simple filters (e.g., list all calls taken yesterday in my call center, list all sale transactions made by my team so far today, list all General Ledger transactions or Journal Entries this month).

OLAP

Online analytical processing (OLAP) is frequently referred to as "cubes." It is an approach that offers data in preaggregated form. This structure is particularly important in offering not only great performance but great flexibility to interactive dashboards.

Take the foregoing payroll expenses as an example: we can build an OLAP database that gives the cash management manager the total sum of payroll expenses for the pay period. But the same OLAP database can also give the accountant the ability to see the total forecast for the year and drill down to each division or department or month (see the business inquiries from OLAP in Exhibit 9.3). This is where performance and flexibility meet.

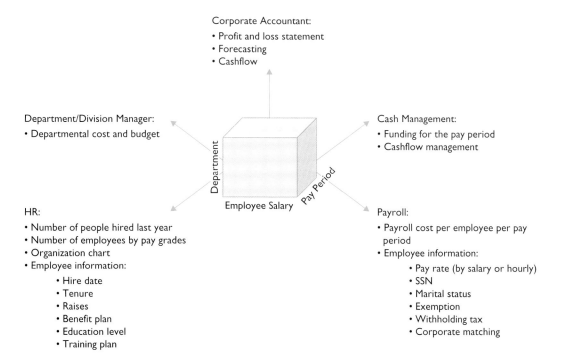

Corporate Accountant:
• Profit and loss statement
• Forecasting
• Cashflow

Department/Division Manager:
• Departmental cost and budget

Cash Management:
• Funding for the pay period
• Cashflow management

Department

Employee Salary   Pay Period

HR:
• Number of people hired last year
• Number of employees by pay grades
• Organization chart
• Employee information:
    • Hire date
    • Tenure
    • Raises
    • Benefit plan
    • Education level
    • Training plan

Payroll:
• Payroll cost per employee per pay period
• Employee information:
    • Pay rate (by salary or hourly)
    • SSN
    • Marital status
    • Exemption
    • Withholding tax
    • Corporate matching

EXHIBIT 9.3 Business Inquiries from OLAP

Such preaggregated data is organized into dimensions (or groupings). An OLAP database, with its dimensions and hierarchies, can offer hundreds or even thousands of variations of aggregations. This type of database plays a very important role in the development of business intelligence, as it provides the foundation for "drill downs." With the ability to drill down or drill up, a chart becomes an interactive object. You can answer many questions from just one component of the dashboard, instead of having to click through many fixed reports.

In addition to offering navigation benefits, an OLAP also offers the possibility for "analysis" (i.e., it continues to find new questions based on old answers). This type of database can quickly answer questions such as "how many people did we hire last year," or "what was our sales in the last five years." However, when you ask the question "how many people did we hire last year," there are many possible follow-up questions—for example, "which department hired more people than the others," "who are the managers that hired these people," "did we hire more than expected," or "what would happen if we had not hired these people," and so on. All these questions can be answered within one OLAP database. See the diagram in Exhibit 9.4 to follow the decision tree.

To answer all these questions, one would write at least five separate queries against the OLTP or ODS and still may not get the answers to some of the questions. But a well-constructed OLAP database can answer all these questions, and quickly.

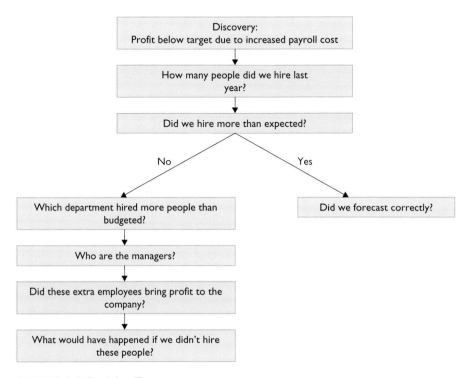

EXHIBIT 9.4 Decision Tree

Dimensions and Facts

An OLAP database is constructed with dimensions and facts. "Facts" are the measurable items (e.g., amount or quantity); thus, facts are also referred to as measures. We would preaggregate facts to answer business questions (e.g., total count of employees, total payroll expenses, etc.). A dimension is the grouping of the fact (e.g., total count of employees "by hire-date," or total payroll expenses "by pay period"). A dimension may contain a hierarchy or multiple hierarchies. These hierarchies allow people to drill from bird's-eye view all the way to the finest grain of details. For example, one may want to see the total number of employees, then break down by the year when they were hired, then break down by quarters, then by months, then by date. This sequence, from year to quarter to month to date, is a hierarchy of the hire-date dimension. It may also be referred to as a "drill-path."

A dimension may have multiple hierarchies to offer people different paths to analyze their data. For example, some people may want to see drill-down from year to half-year to month, while others may want to drill down from year to weeks to dates. Compared to a relational database schema, an OLAP database with a simple time dimension and one fact may already offer many more ways to view the data. (Optionally, the ODS itself may be structured in dimensions and facts as to provide the foundation on which to form OLAP databases.)

How do we build an OLAP? Let us follow the foregoing thinking pattern. In order to answer the first question "did we hire more than expected," we would quickly realize we need a Scenario dimension. A Scenario dimension is usually used for actual versus budget scenarios. In this case, we would have the "expected" scenario versus what actually happened. By now, we have two dimensions, "time" and "scenario," and one fact, "employee count."

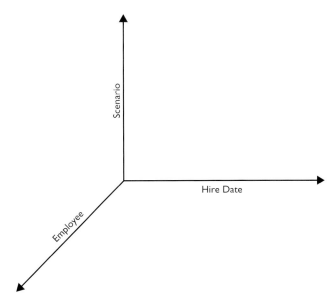

EXHIBIT 9.5 Forming a Cube

If we take apart "employee count" and separate it into a fact and a dimension (i.e., fact is the quantity and add a dimension as "employee"), we would have a three-dimensional database, otherwise known as a "cube" (see Exhibit 9.5). We can begin to query this three-dimensional database by any interception of the three dimensions. For example, actual employees hired in January 2008 versus budgeted would produce the following result:

Newly Hired Employees in January 2008

HIRE DATE	JANUARY 2008	
	ACTUAL	BUDGET
Number of Employees	25	20

Furthermore, employees may be grouped into departments or their managers. Now we can answer questions such as "how many employees did we hire last year," as well as "which departments were they in," and "who are their managers," all from one database. The following are report examples:

Newly Hired Employees in January 2008, by Department

HIRE DATE:	JANUARY 2008
SCENARIO:	ACTUAL
Finance Department	3
Human Resources Department	7
Sales Department	15

Newly Hired Employees in January 2008, by Department Manager

HIRE DATE:	JANUARY 2008
SCENARIO:	ACTUAL
Jim Jones	3
Joe Smith	7
Janet Johnson	15

Newly Hired Employees in January 2008, by Departments and Managers

HIRE DATE:	JANUARY 2008	
SCENARIO:	ACTUAL	
Finance Department	Jim Jones	3
Human Resources Department	Joe Smith	7
Sales Department	Janet Johnson	15

Actual versus Budget—Newly Hired by Departments and Managers

HIRE DATE:	JANUARY 2008	ACTUAL	BUDGET
Finance Department	Jim Jones	3	0
Human Resources Department	Joe Smith	7	0
Sales Department	Janet Johnson	15	15

These reports, if based on a relational database, would have to be built one by one, and each query might have to join different tables together. But using OLAP, we would need only one OLAP database to offer for all these reports. Because of this capability, many queries built on OLAP are typically dynamic queries (i.e., they offer end-users the flexibility to drill to wherever they wish).

From the example provided, even though Janet Johnson, the sales department manager, hired the most people in January, she did not exceed her budget. It was Jim and Joe in the finance and human resources departments who exceeded their budgeted head counts. However, we can realize this only at the "Actual versus Budget—Newly Hired by Departments and Managers" report. If this report were not available, then the chief operating officer (COO) might have a false impression of Janet's hiring behavior. With OLAP, the COO could drag any dimension to column heading or row heading or filter sections, could drill down or drill cross, on the fly, depending on where the analysis takes him or her.

ROLAP and Star Schema

Transforming the OLTP's relational database schema to a star schema is the first step toward building an OLAP database. A simple star schema basically has a single fact table at the center. The dimensional foreign keys on this fact table then exchange with the primary keys of each dimension table while forming a star (see examples of star schema in Exhibits 9.6 and 9.7).

A relational OLAP (ROLAP) is a database structure that organizes databases on the star schema. Information on ROLAP would be prestructured by dimensions and facts. ROLAP databases are stored in relational tables, which

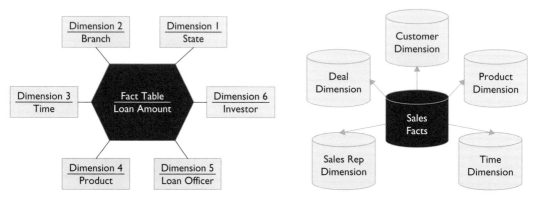

EXHIBIT 9.6 Star Schema: Example 1

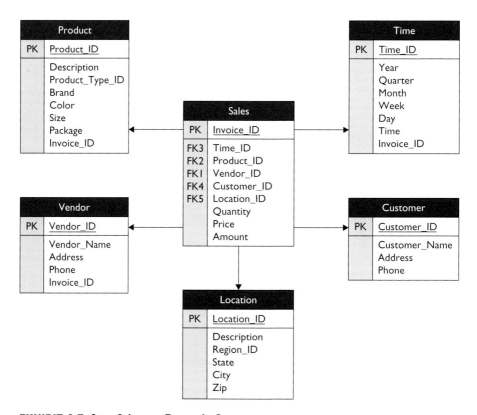

EXHIBIT 9.7 Star Schema: Example 2

can be queried using standard SQL scripts. There is still a small latency between OLTP and ROLAP because of the restructuring of data. Usually the data load is incremental, in order to reduce the load time.

A ROLAP database is used usually for larger dimensions (i.e., many dimension members). For example, in a manufacturing company, the "Products" dimension may contain thousands of SKUs (Stock-keeping units) or a call center cube may contain hundreds or thousands of "Customers." If people want to drill down to an SKU level or an individual customer level, then the data should be kept in ROLAP format. Additionally, if a dimension has many attributes, it should be kept in ROLAP. An attribute is the information of a dimension member. For example, a customer normally would have an address that contains city, state, and zip code. A customer record would also have information such as Primary-Contact, or Purchase Volume, or the Sales Region to which it belongs, or the Service Region to which it belongs. The city, state, zip code, primary contact, purchase volume, sales region, and service region are the "attributes" of a customer. Attributes can also be used in queries (e.g., total sales amounts for all customers in the state of California). This query filters on "customer" dimension's "state" attribute. However, one may query on "average" sales amount for all customers in the state of California, or "maximum" sales amount in California, or "minimum" sales amount in California. In order to preaggregate and store all these values, the database would quickly grow very large, especially when there are thousands of customers in the dimension. Therefore, attribute aggregations are usually calculated "on demand" when the dashboard queries the data. For the same storage concerns, when there are many attributes for one member (one customer) we would keep the database in a ROLAP structure.

Materialized Query

While Materialized Query Table (MQT) or Views are not really in the OLAP family, the underlying structure is actually very similar to ROLAP structure. Materialize Query Table is a term defined by IBM, and Materialized Query Views (MQVs) are by Oracle. The two technologies are very similar and use very similar scripts. Basically, these are trigger-based data replications, and they store the aggregation physically. The way it works is that you create a table with aggregations. For example, you originally have a MQT containing the following:

Customer	Sales Rep	Month of Sales	Sales Amount
ABC Company	John	Jan 2008	2,000.00
CDE Company	Joe	Jan 2008	1,500.00
EFG Company	John	Feb 2008	350.00

When the source system's trigger sends a new transaction, it looks like the following:

Customer	Sales Rep	Sales Date	Sales Amount
CDE Co.	Joe	Jan 28, 2008	4,500.00

The system keeps a snapshot of the original table: Joe sold $1500.00 in January to CDE Co. Then, the system transforms and adds the new transaction to meet the Month format.

Customer	Sales Rep	Sales Date	Sales Amount
CDE Co.	Joe	Jan, 2008	4,500.00

The system then identifies the matching row from the original MQT.

Customer	Sales Rep	Month of Sales	Sales Amount	
CDE Co.	Joe	Jan 2008	1,500.00	* Original transaction
CDE Co.	Joe	Jan 2008	4,500.00	* Newly added transaction

Adding the original and new transactions together produces a higher sales amount for Joe in January.

Customer	Sales Rep	Month of Sales	Sales Amount
ABC Co.	John	Jan 2008	2,000.00
CDE Co.	Joe	Jan 2008	6,000.00
EFG Co.	John	Feb 2008	350.00

There are numerous ways to refresh and optimize these MQT/MQVs. While MQT/MQVs seem simple and comparable to relational database structure, much more system resources are required to maintain the trigger-based synchronizations.

DOLAP

DOLAP stands for Desktop OLAP. This type of OLAP is usually built by end users. They would download a data set (usually onto Excel) and then build pivot tables on this data set. The pivot table allows them to filter from one column to another, similar to drilling from one dimension to another. They can also drill down to details, which are the transactional data from within the data set. This type of database has structure similar to that of ROLAP, but in much smaller scale and designed by end-users on their own workstations.

MOLAP and Snowflake Schema

MOLAP stands for Multi-dimensional OLAP. In many ways, MOLAP is very similar to ROLAP. Both are built on dimensions and facts, and both are scripted for aggregations. A major difference is data storage. MOLAP stores the dimensional aggregated results, whereas ROLAP stores dimensions and facts tables (to get the results, we would have to join the dimension and facts tables together). With this major difference, MOLAP tends to aggregate data into a higher level, in order to use hard disk space efficiently. Also, because of the stored values, MOLAP would accommodate a "snowflake" schema (see Exhibit 9.8 for examples). Generally, if we build SQL scripts to link tables together per snowflake schema, the query would be very slow.

However, in MOLAP, we do not have to join the tables. We simply feed each table into the dimensional hierarchy one by one. As long as each data load contains both the parent column and the child column, we can build the hierarchy one layer at a time, while each time we need only two columns. Take the chart in Exhibit 9.8 as an example; the Time dimension is built by three tables, and each has only one to two columns. A more complex example in Exhibit 9.9 shows that you would have one table for product items, and the item's supplier is linked to another table called "supplier." In this case, we have a dimension's attribute linking to another dimension, allowing people to use Supplier to filter the product items. This "dimensional link" is a special characteristic of a snowflake schema.

MOLAP differs from ROLAP in its use of the snowflake schema. ROLAP allows drilldown to transactional level—thus the database schema would not be too complicated. MOLAP, however, stores aggregations on an upper level, thus allowing more complicated schema. One may consider MOLAP as a consolidated form of multiple ROLAPs.

MOLAP certainly has higher latency than ROLAP, but it delivers better query performance to dashboards, especially for senior management.

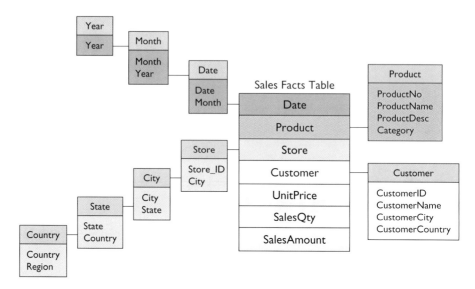

EXHIBIT 9.8 Snowflake Schema: Example 1

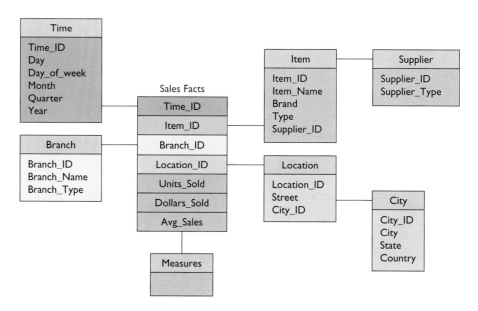

EXHIBIT 9.9 Snowflake Schema: Example 2

HOLAP

Hybrid OLAP (HOLAP) takes advantage of both ROLAP and MOLAP technologies. It usually requires dimensional mapping from ROLAP to MOLAP. This offers the great performance and complex attributes of MOLAP, along with the ability to drill down to much lower transactional details on ROLAP.

Conformed Dimensions

What are conformed dimensions?

> A conformed dimension is a set of data attributes that have been physically implemented in multiple database tables using the same structure, attributes, domain values, definitions and concepts in each implementation.
>
> —DATA-WAREHOUSES.NET

What does this mean? And why do we want to have conformed dimensions? Refer back to the HOLAP concept discussed previously.

Assuming we have multiple ROLAPs, each derived from a different data source, and they all have a dimension called "Customer." We may already have several dashboard-built bases on these ROLAPs. Now, we want to build a MOLAP to combine all these ROLAPs together but only to store the top two levels. How can we consolidate these ROLAPs if Customer dimensions in the ROLAPs contain different hierarchies? We cannot.

Technical issues aside, having conformed dimensions also gives dashboards unified navigation. Regardless of which dashboard is used, people would always see the same things (i.e., they would always drill down from Customer Group, to Customer's first initial, to Customer Name). They do not have to guess.

Now that we understand that whatever OLAP database we build may always be referenced later, we should always build our OLAPs with such expansion in mind. For example, assume we are building a Sales OLAP. During our project assessment, we know we need to build a Customer dimension, and each customer would be rolled up to "Region." Also, during the assessment, we know that the Customer table in the source system is actually shared by many other departments, such as the Service department, but they roll up customers to a "Service Region." So, even though our initial project is only for the Sales department, we should be aware that our Customer dimension may be reused in the future by the Service department. We should name the Region level as "Sales Region" so that it is not confused with the "Service Region" later. The end result of this "Customer" dimension would accommodate drill-down from "Customer Initials" to "Customer ID," with "Sales Region" (and "Service Region") as an attribute. This is how we can take advantage of the Conformed Dimension.

DATA MARTS

A data mart is a collection of subject areas organized for decision support based on the needs of a given department. . . . There are two kinds of data marts—dependent and independent. A dependent data mart is one whose source is a data warehouse. An independent data mart is one whose source is the legacy applications environment. All dependent data marts are fed by the same source—the data warehouse. Each independent data mart is fed uniquely and separately by the legacy applications environment. Dependent data marts are architecturally and structurally sound. Independent data marts are unstable and architecturally unsound, at least for the long haul.

—Bill Inmon[4]

We can consider data marts as being a slice of the MOLAP/ROLAP, or a filtered section of the ODS. There may be additional transformations to customize the data, tailored to end users' terminology.

Notes

1. Bill Inmon, "Tech Topic: What is Data Warehouse," *Prism Solutions*, 1995.
2. Bill Inmon, "The Operational Data Store," *InfoDB magazine*, February 1995.
3. Bill Inmon, "The Operational Data Store, Designing the Operational Data Store," *DM Review*, July 1998.
4. Bill Inmon, "Data Mart Does Not Equal Data Warehouse," *DM Direct,* November 1999 (http://www.dmreview.com/dmdirect/19991120/1675-1.html).

Data Replication and Delivery

10

Now that we understand the various structures to host our data, let us look at how we put data into them.

ETL

ETL stands for "Extract, Transform and Load." It is a process to take data from one system to another, frequently in the context of building a data warehouse.

The extraction of data from a source system would require a good software driver that can establish the connection between the source and the ETL tool. Frequently, a SQL-based ETL tool would use some kind of Open Database Connectivity (ODBC) driver. A more efficient ETL tool would use whatever the native drivers are to connect to the source systems, which reduces much of the system overhead.

As we know, most source systems are not "report friendly." For example, most financial systems store the data in tables with very cryptic names (e.g., F0411, G2948). Likewise, the field names are equally cryptic (e.g., AG0402, GL7362, etc.). When replicating data from this type of systems, transformation is inevitable. No business users would be able to understand their income statements if it contains labels such as AG0402 or GL7362. Whatever data is stored in the reporting systems should always reference user-friendly terms (e.g., General Ledger, Asset Depreciation, Sales Order, etc.). Systematically, there would be a process to transcribe F0411 to "General Ledger," F1201 to "Asset Depreciation," and AG0402 to "Department," or "0/1" to "male/female."

This is why we need the "transformation" layer, which is usually the layer that people do not see and do not even know about.

Once the source data has been transformed to user-friendly terms, it needs to go into the target system. Again, we need to have some kind of driver to connect to the target system and feed data into it in the format that it can understand. Some ETL tools contain a set of drivers that can read and send data across platforms, which would change CCSID or language settings on the fly. The more intelligent the drivers, the better the data load. Ideally, the end result in the target system would contain data that end users can directly query and can fully understand.

There are many scripting methods that help to reduce resource consumption and shorten data-load time. For example, you would want to filter before joining (i.e., instead of joining two large tables and then applying filters at the result, it is faster to prefilter these tables to get smaller data sets before you join them together). This is because the filter is applied to the entire table, whereas the "join" command has to find the matching row. Also, consider issuing "Delete" and "Insert" commands instead of "Update," because the "Update" command searches and matches the exact row, whereas "Delete" and "Insert" commands are applied to a data set. Generally speaking, as long as you know which commands are row based and which are dataset-based, you are likely to write economical ETL scripts.

METADATA AND MDM

Metadata is "data about data." A metadata repository contains the key information on how to translate the source database. Master Data Management (MDM) is a system containing collections of metadata, system connections, the transformations, and more. Metadata and MDMs do not usually store data itself; they store only the ingredients necessary for the process. For example, MDM would contain the data mapping and translation of each table and all fields. Sometimes, MDM may also contain the data attributes. More advanced MDM tools would even keep the target mapping of these data columns (e.g., target database, dimension mapping, etc.).

When building a data warehouse, the MDM, or a repository of metadata, helps greatly to bring together the source systems, the ODS, and the OLAP. It provides the entire audit trail of transformation.

SERVICE-ORIENTED ARCHITECTURE

While traditional data warehouse techniques focus on physical data transfers, there are many newer methods utilizing virtual data warehouse techniques. The physical data replications are accomplished by some type of ETL process to copy data from one database to another, while transforming data en route. The virtual methods transmit and receive XML messages between two web servers, generally referred to as enterprise application integration (EAI) or enterprise information integration (EII), which are built on service-oriented architecture (SOA).

SOA is another form of architecture supporting the process of data integration. The "service" in this case refers to web services. This architecture builds on the open platform of the web interface to send data from the source to the target system. The package, also referred to as a "message," is usually in the form of XML. This method of delivery no longer requires database-specific drivers. However, it still needs some kind of common understanding between the source and the target systems, such as the mapping of fields or the data types. This commonality is built on several components: XML DTD (Data Type Definition), SOAP protocol, and Web Service Description Language (WSDL). Sometimes, these XML messages may be formatted in such a way that they are delivered directly to dashboards, which achieve a real-time or near-real-time delivery. The SOA method of delivery usually contains minimal transformation. Rather, the source data would have been pretransformed before being delivered. There is also a confirmation response from the target system, keeping the replication in sync. IBM Message Queue (MQ) Series is an example of this SOA method. The message queue contains the list of messages and the status of the transmission.

The characteristics of SOA are as follows:

- Web-based open platform
- Real-time delivery
- Small package–enhanced User Interface delivery performance.

SOA is a great method especially when delivering fixed results on a web-based interface. Along with more and more common design platforms, such as Eclipse, Java, C++, C#, .NET, and so on, it has become the standard choice of delivery by many reporting tools.

However, SOA is not limited to ETL and data transfer. SOA is an architecture. More and more business intelligence (BI) tools are now building on web services rather the traditional client-server model. These BI tools leverage the web server services (e.g., Microsoft Internet Information Services, or IBM Websphere web server) to deliver the .xml packages to dashboards. Many dashboard tools also leverage on the foundation available on the web servers (e.g., .Net Frameworks, AJAX, etc.) to offer even greater interactivity and flexibility. However, SOA, as a data delivery method, may not eliminate the need for ETL and the data warehouse. Frequently, under a large, complex environment, we still need to ETL the OLTP data into ODS and/or a data warehouse before sending the .xml into dashboards.

Query Language and Interactivity

11

D ifferent database structures require different query languages. The most common language is Structured Query Language (SQL). SQL queries the relational online transaction processing (OLTP) and operational data store (ODS) databases, whereas Multi-dimensional Scripting (MDX) is the language to interface with online analytical processing (OLAP) cubes specifically. MDX is a query language, one that is also used in scripting many functionalities of the OLAP cubes.

SQL

Many people are familiar with the SQL language, which has been a standard query language for relational databases for many years. Although there have been several standards and platforms, overall, the language still conforms to the same general structure. Minimally, a SQL statement requires the following two clauses:

1. Select
2. From

The "Select" clause indicates the columns you choose to display, and the "From" clause indicates the table or view the columns come from. In addition, there are optional clauses such as "Where," "Order By," "Group By," "Having," and so on. You can also "join" tables together to make a larger set.

There are several standard functions already defined in SQL. For example, the "Year" function returns the year of a date and the "Sum" function is an aggregation function, adding up the values in a column.

The following is an example of a SQL statement:

```
Select

    p.[ProductGroup], year(s.[SalesDate]) as [Yr], c.[Continent],
    sum(s.[SalesAmt]) as [sumSalesAmt]

From

    [tblSales] s

    Join [tblProduct] p on s.[ProductID] = p.[ProductID]

    Join [tblRegion] c on s.[RegionID] = c.[RegionID]

Where

    p.[ProductGroup] = `Computers`

    and year(s.[SalesDate]) between 1996 and 1997

Group by

    p.[ProductGroup], c.[Continent], year(s.[SalesDate])

Order by

    1, 2, 3
```

This SQL statement returns the following result:

[ProductGroup]	[Yr]	[Continent]	[sumSalesAmt]
Computers	1996	Africa	127,359
Computers	1996	America	570,351
Computers	1996	Australia	259,337
Computers	1996	Asia	437,594
Computers	1996	Europe	372,495
Computers	1997	Africa	136,704
Computers	1997	America	673,544
Computers	1997	Australia	302,482
Computers	1997	Asia	535,780
Computers	1997	Europe	437,507

MDX

MDX stands for "Multi-Dimensional Scripting" language. Like SQL, it is a query language. But in this case, it is used to retrieve data from OLAP databases instead. Many dashboard tools that offer the drilling capability actually contain MDX scripts underneath. Given that each OLAP has multiple dimensions and each dimension contains many levels and members, an MDX must therefore reference dimensions and members to clearly identify each member (or "node"). If the member exists in many levels, the MDX also needs to reference the level name. There are many functions that work with MDX, as with SQL scripts. Most importantly you should understand the "parent and child" relationship: a "parent" is the aggregation of all its "children," "Year" is the parent of "Quarter." "Quarter" is a parent of "Month." "Year" is an ancestor of "Month." The lowest level in a dimension is referred to as "Leaves," a metaphor from a tree structure. The result of an MDX script can be a data cell or a range of data. Either way, it would minimally specify the column heading and the row heading, and it sometimes includes a "slicer" in the "where" clause (similar to a SQL filter). The following is a generic select statement in MDX script:

```
SELECT { Years.[1996], Years.[1997] } ON COLUMNS,

Regions.Continents.members ON ROWS

FROM Sales

WHERE (Products.[Product Group].[Computers] )
```

This script produces the following result:

Computers		
	1996	1997
Africa	127,359	136,704
America	570,351	673,544
Australia	259,337	302,482
Asia	437,594	535,780
Europe	372,495	437,507

Note the similarity and the difference between the results from SQL versus those from MDX. The MDX column heading can expand horizontally to include more years, whereas SQL column headings are fixed. Many people see this format as a "pivot table." Yes, the result of an MDX is a pivot table. In fact, when Microsoft SQL Server started to incorporate the OLAP technique, one of the required server services was the "Pivot Table Service." Its main function was to preaggregate the transactions in relational tables. This pivot table format helps greatly in establishing the graphical nature of dashboards.

A bar chart, for example, shows a comparison of the many values side by side, so you can quickly spot which value is higher than others. It is composed of an x and a y axis. To display such a bar chart, the data behind it must also contain *x*- and *y*-axis labels. Let us take a look at the MDX pivot table result, shown as follows:

Computers		
	1996	1997
Africa	127,359	136,704
America	570,351	673,544
Australia	259,337	302,482
Asia	437,594	535,780
Europe	372,495	437,507

The columns "1996" and "1997" and the row headings "Africa," "America," and so on would naturally fit into the *x*- and *y*-axes. In fact, we have two choices: the continents may be on the *x*-axis or the *y*-axis (see Exhibit 11.1). In the first bar chart, we can see the comparison of the continents within each year, and it shows that the American continent has the highest sales amount for both years. In the second bar chart, we can see the comparison of the continents against each other as well as the annual amounts within each continent. Not only does America have the highest Sales for both years, but it is growing.

Now, let us use the SQL result to see whether we can produce the same graphs (see Exhibit 11.2). We still have the same ten bars, but each bar is now separate and has its own color. They are no longer grouped by continent

Computers		
	1996	1997
Africa	127,359	136,704
America	570,351	673,544
Australia	259,337	302,482
Asia	437,594	535,780
Europe	372,495	437,507

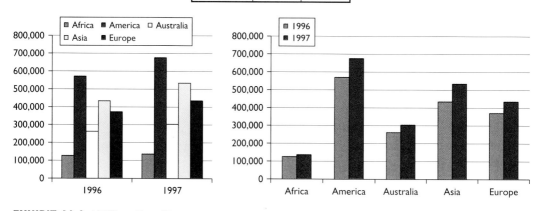

EXHIBIT 11.1 MDX to Bar Charts

[ProductGroup]	[Yr]	[Continent]	[sumSalesAmt]
Computers	1996	Afirca	127,359
Computers	1996	America	570,351
Computers	1996	Australia	259,337
Computers	1996	Asia	437,594
Computers	1996	Europe	372,495
Computers	1997	Afirca	136,704
Computers	1997	America	673,544
Computers	1997	Australia	302,482
Computers	1997	Asia	535,780
Computers	1997	Europe	437,507

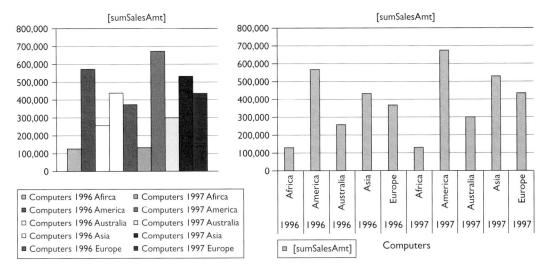

EXHIBIT 11.2 SQL to Bar Chart

or year. In this setting, we cannot compare year to year, or continent to continent. Which continent has the most sales? We do not know! So far, we have used only one chart type, the bar chart, as an example to compare the results of MDX versus SQL. What happens when we have more complicated charts to display, such as stacked-bar charts, multiple-area charts, bubble charts, and so on?

SQL script, although it has its uses, is not a very effective way to translate to charts and graphs. Aside from the apparent performance reasons, this is also why we would design OLAP and MDX before we design dashboards.

DRILL UP, DRILL DOWN, DRILL ACROSS, DRILL TO DETAIL

One major benefit of building an OLAP is that it gives dashboard users the capability to view information in multiple ways (e.g., drill up, drill down, drill across, or drill anywhere).

Drill up or drill down means that users can see the aggregated numbers in the upper level or the lower level very quickly. Drill down is used to display the supplemental layer of the displayed information, following the dimension hierarchy from upper level summary to lower details; drill up is used to follow the dimension hierarchy from the lower details to the upper summary. Take the Customer dimension, for example: we can drill up from Customer Names to Customer Sales Region, or drill down from a Customer Sales Region to Customer Names—all from the same chart object.

Another benefit of OLAP is the capability to drill across. Drill across means we can drill from one dimension to another. For example, when you see the "total sales amount by customers," you may want to see the products sold to a certain customer. Drilling from the Customer dimension to the Products dimension is a form of drill across. Not all dashboard tools can accommodate the drill across function.

Drill to detail is used to see the lowest level of the OLAP that makes up the total amounts. Some tools also offer "drill through," which means you can leave the OLAP database to see the transactions from the source relational system. Keep in mind that although the lowest level in an OLAP may be the detail transactions, sometimes that is not the case. Also, most extract-transform-load processes have a time delay. So drill to detail may not show the same result as drill through. Again, not all dashboard tools can offer these functions.

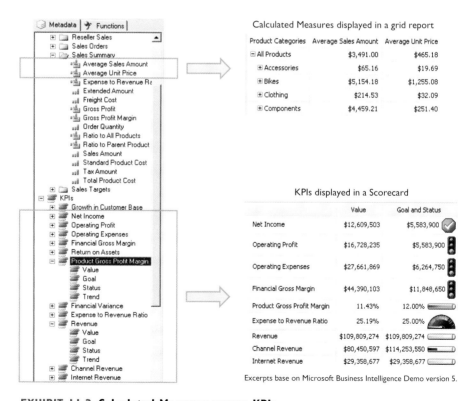

EXHIBIT 11.3 Calculated Measures versus KPIs
Excerpts based on Microsoft Business Intelligence Demo, version 5

KEY PERFORMANCE INDICATORS

A key performance indicator (KPI) is a metric used to measure the core success of the company's performance. Frequently, the KPIs are at a very high level and somewhat intangible. They are usually ratios of certain measures. Inevitably we have to calculate KPIs after the majority of the base measures have been made available.

For some people, creating a KPI is done by (1) creating a KPI member and (2) setting KPI member value = measure A/measure B. In this case, the term "KPI" is similar to "calculated cube measures". They appear identical to regular measures and can be queried just like a regular measure. See Chapter 5 regarding the difference between metrics and KPIs.

However, sometimes a KPI, because of its special purpose, may also contain additional attributes, which sets it apart from a calculated measure. As a data warehouse designer, not only can you preset both the KPI's calculation, but also its trending and indicator, and so on. In essence, you can determine not only the KPI's value but its look and feel, regardless of what the front-end tool is. See Exhibit 11.3 on the difference between calculated measures and KPIs on a Microsoft SQL Server.

Data Warehouse and Business Intelligence Dashboard Paradigm

12

While understanding the data architecture is important, we should not lose sight of what we design it for. Learning from all the failed business intelligence (BI) projects, it should be apparent that the makeup of the data warehouse should tightly integrate with users' requests—otherwise, it defeats the purpose of having one.

The downside in building a data warehouse is its latency. Whenever we talk about building a separate system to keep the same data, we have to replicate the data from one system to another. Sometimes, it takes only microseconds, such as with High Availability Systems; other times, it is scheduled monthly, such as with many of the online analytical processing (OLAP) processes; and sometimes, it is on demand per users' request. Regardless of the method used, there is always some degree of delay. After all, not only are we copying the data from one system to another, we are also rearranging and sometimes changing the data. The question is, then, how do we balance the format of the data and the delivery performance? It seems that the closer the query is to the source system, the shorter the latency of the report delivery; or the better the data structure can meet the report demands, the more time it takes to prepare the data.

This is why whenever we start a dashboard project we should always ask "how quickly do you want to see the data?" Frequently, users say "I want it real time." However, what does "real time" really mean? If people enter data into the source system only four or five times a day, why would we need to load it into a data warehouse every minute? If our source system gets updates by some sort of batch process, how would it be possible for us to provide real-time dashboards? As we ask further about the business purposes or how frequently the data changes, the "real time" may become "every five minutes" or "every hour" or even "next day." After all, most data in the source system does not change in microseconds (except for e-commerce systems).

Sometimes, people ask for "real-time" data not because they want it in real time, but because they do not know when the data is changed. Then, our efforts should be on "how can we know when the data has been updated" instead of "how frequently should we load data". In some cases, the data does not change frequently, but when it does get updated, it is critical that it be known immediately. In this case, we should take advantage of the real-time delivery on triggered SOA (Service Oriented Architecture).

A business dashboard contains many charts and graphs. Each chart offers a perspective that other charts do not. Some charts have a very short time window, whereas other charts cover multiple years of information; some charts are very focused within one small geographical area, whereas other charts cover the entire globe. Because these charts offer different perspectives, they may come from different data sources or from the same source but organized in different ways. In order to offer data effectively, we need to organize the underlying data as it is organized in the dashboards. In other words, we would want to reverse-engineer the dashboard to design our data warehouse. There are many ways to go about doing so. One very common method is using the "time" variance. In this case, the time variance would refer to the different refresh rate requirement of each chart (i.e., how soon do people want to see their charts after the data becomes available).

As discussed in Part 1, there are three major types of dashboards—strategic, tactical, and operational. Each type of dashboard is intended for a different purpose. In addition, different roles may require data with different latency (e.g., real-time versus short-range versus long-range dashboards).

REAL-TIME DASHBOARDS

A real-time dashboard contains shorter time ranges and sometimes a brief aggregation of raw transactional data. An example of such a real-time dashboard would be a Network Traffic Dashboard (Exhibit 12.1). This dashboard shows the network traffic within a one-hour window; it tells you which ten machines "talk" the most and indicates the network utilization, number of packets per second, and number of errors per second as of now. If there is any file that is taking up most of the bandwidth, it will also display the file. This dashboard has a specific purpose—monitoring the network activities as

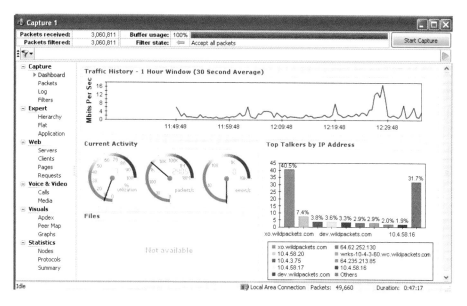

EXHIBIT 12.1 Network Traffic Dashboard
Source: http://www.wildpackets.com/products/omnipeek/enterprise_overview/features_dashboard_view

they are happening. It not only tells you how your network is performing, but, more importantly, it tells you when your network is bogged down. When there are excessive collisions, it also tells you which machine may be the culprit.

Another example of real-time delivery is alerts. Alerts are a type of component within a dashboard. They usually contain only one phrase (e.g., "Red Sox won"). It is a quick note that monitors one single event. This type of alert originally showed up in various dashboards (e.g., "Sales up 30% today" or "MTD Sales 10% exceed target"). However, when personal digital assistants (PDAs) became more and more popular and the technology more mature, these alerts were delivered to PDAs and the alerts appeared in real-time delivery.

This type of dashboard can pull data directly from the transactional systems or the operational data store and deliver it as an .xml message or as a queried data set.

SHORT-RANGE DASHBOARDS

A dashboard that displays daily information is typically used to monitor Week-to-Date, Month-to-Date, Quarter-to-Date, or Year-to-Date progressions. This type of data is frequently displayed in operational dashboards.

An operational dashboard helps managers understand their daily operations from various views and angles. This type of dashboard usually includes

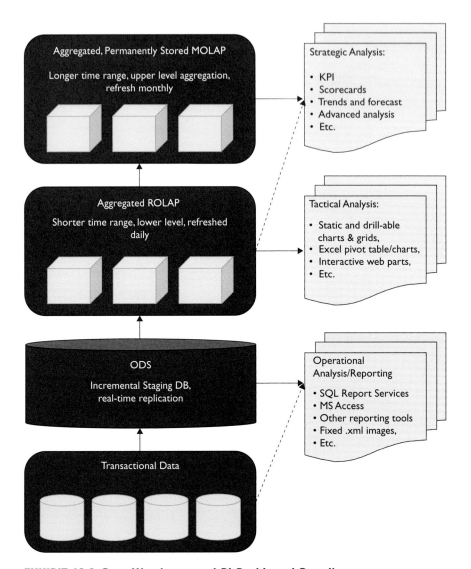

EXHIBIT 12.2 Data Warehouse and BI Dashboard Paradigm

many charts and graphs. One major characteristic of an operational dashboard is that it combines data from multiple data sources. So we usually would want to build a data mart for this type of dashboard. In this data mart, we would precombine and preaggregate the source data in order to enhance the dashboard's performance. Sometimes, the users of these dashboards will require "drill-to-detail" capability, in order to view the supporting transactional data for justifications or discoveries. A Relational OLAP (ROLAP) would be better suited to offer data for this type of dashboard.

LONG-RANGE DASHBOARDS

A dashboard that contains a longer time range is usually called a strategic dashboard. Such a dashboard would contain higher-level calculations and key performance indicators (KPIs). Raw data directly from the transactional systems would not usually suffice. In order to offer optimal performance, we would build Multi-Dimensional OLAP (MOLAP) databases for these. A MOLAP database stores aggregated values, thus enabling upper-level calculations, such as those for KPIs.

Exhibit 12.2 demonstrates the connection between data warehouse structures and the different types of dashboards.

USE CASES

Now that you have a good general understanding of the various techniques available to build the dashboard foundation, let us take a look at the various dashboards to see how they are made:

Example 1. The Scorecards in the use case shown in Chapter 6 (Exhibit 6.1): The purpose of a balanced scorecard is to monitor the activities within various departments to ensure that they are strategically aligned. You would want to take the activities throughout a longer period of time to see the progress correctly. Thus, scorecards are usually derived from MOLAP databases, which preaggregate the detail transactions and store upper-level calculated KPIs.

Example 2. Monthly gross margin by regions bar charts in the use case shown in Chapter 6 (Exhibits 6.2 through 6.8): Gross Margin is Gross Profit divided by Sales Revenue. These charts show no reference to Gross Profit or Sales Revenue, which means Gross Margins are a precalculated and stored value (thus they can be independently queried and displayed). Additionally, users can drill down from Regions to Countries and to Cities to see that Bonn has the lowest margin and then drill across to Product to find that Hydrating Pack is the failed product. These interactivities show the underlying database is most likely some form of online analytical processing (OLAP). These two telltale signs—precalculated and stored values and drillable dimensions—let us know that the underlying database is a MOLAP. If the bar chart displays Revenue instead of Gross Margin, it is possible the underlying database is a ROLAP instead. Revenue is a simple sum aggregation. Thus, it may be dynamically calculated and delivered to dashboards.

Example 3. The real-time dashboard shown in Exhibit 12.1: This dashboard has a [Start Capture] button on the top-right corner. It allows users to decide when they will begin to capture network packets. When the packets have been captured, the captured packets are displayed according to various categorizations, based on the type of activities, the machine addresses, the machine type, and so forth. Most likely there is a database (as simple as a log) somewhere serving this dashboard. The database would be empty initially, and begins to fill up only when someone clicks on [Start Capture]. There is no latency to speak of. All information must be displayed immediately within microseconds. The dashboard offers no capability to drill. This tells us that the underlying database is most likely a direct relational database storing every transaction (packet) received. The aggregations are calculated on the fly.

Mobile Business Intelligence

13

Mobile business intelligence (BI) is BI delivered to mobile devices, such as cell phones and personal digital assistants (PDAs). Mobile devices, given their fundamental purpose, should be small and portable. Accordingly, they have small-sized screens. Thus the dashboards we develop for desktops or laptops may not display very well on these small devices. So, we have to come up with ingenious ways to deliver the same "intelligent" information on a smaller scale.

Aside from the small screen size, cell phone technologies vary greatly. The "Palm" operating system has dominated the PDA market for years, and it was one of the first to incorporate PDA and cell phone technologies. At the same time, Hewlett-Packard had its similar version of "smart phone." However, it did not take long before BlackBerry, Microsoft, Apple, and others all developed their versions of smart phones. While each company developed its own mobile methodology, they all tried to achieve the same thing—to bring pertinent information to users as quickly as possible when the users are away from their computers. Consider the importance of BI dashboards to a business; it became an essential part of the business function to bring these BI dashboards to mobile devices.

There are two approaches to mobile BI deployments—thick-client and thin-client. Thick-client deployments run special software on each type of mobile device, fed by special servers that manage the interactions with those devices. The client-side software controls how content is displayed. This was an important factor in the early days of mobile browsers, when each device displayed content differently. Most BI vendors offer thick-client solutions, with different client software for the different mobile devices. Their approaches work well for organizations that have settled on a relatively small number of mobile devices. A thin-client solution uses standard Web technologies to deliver and display information. Thus to offer interactive information, the interactivity must be performed on the server side. This method requires a constant connection to the BI server.

Perhaps the more effective method is a combination of both the connected and disconnected modes. When connected, we can interact with the BI objects, drill up or down, drill across, change data source or parameters, and so on. When we find the pertinent information, we should be able to download the results onto a smart phone for future viewing. Optionally, due to the limited memory capabilities, the object may be downloaded with a small embedded data set. In other words, with a live connection, a smart phone can utilize the server's resource to perform dynamic calculations; but without a live connection, a smart phone may perform simple calculations on a much smaller subset of data.

Aside from the limited resources, smart phones are also limited by their screen sizes. To compromise, instead of displaying a full-blown dashboard with multiple charts and graphs, we may be able to display only one chart at a time. This leads to the selection of BI dashboards that can incorporate with mobile devices. If a dashboard contains multiple objects (also referred to as "web parts") and each object is independent of the other, it would migrate to smart phones much more easily, whereas if we have a dashboard containing multiple objects all dependent on each other, it would be difficult to put the entire dependency onto the small display screen of smart phones. So, it would be critical to selectively deploy the BI dashboards onto mobile devices, and some degree of customization may be needed.

Generally speaking, the data architecture designed for dashboards would suffice as the delivery source for smart phones. The only impact is on the delivery methods—mostly Web-service oriented.

PART 2 SUMMARY AND READINESS CHECKLIST

As new technologies evolve, the fine lines between online transaction process, operational data store, data warehouse, data mart, or online analytical process become blurry. More and more tools will be developed to streamline the process to quickly deliver information to users' hands. The process to perform extract-transform-load is always necessary, because of the fundamental difference between an online transaction process system and a reporting system. However, more and more metadata connectors and automation packages will become available, which eliminates the need to custom-build scripts. This is very similar to the precooked packaged frozen dinner in the supermarket. We can just open the box, heat it up, and have a well-proportioned, well-balanced, and delicious dinner.

A movement referred as "Business Intelligence 2.0" or "Second Generation BI" is emerging. This direction of business intelligence (BI) focuses on developing new BI products that are much more user friendly, as they really should be. Looking back at the maturity cycle of BI, several technologies emerged during the past 20 years. We went from fixed reporting to OLAP-based drillable interactive reporting, and from structured data schema to practically any information. The term "Business Intelligence" is becoming much more of a live topic, one that evolves along with our business needs.

Very soon, people will begin to collect the "most commonly used queries" and build repositories of them. Likewise, repositories of KPIs will be available as to build industry standards. Additionally, we will have a tool that can dynamically design the supporting databases according to users' needs. Such a tool will bring BI to a new light, where the tool itself contains its own database intelligence. It will know when to build a multidimensional OLAP, when to build a relational OLAP, and when to keep the data in transactional state, all with optimized indexes and aggregations. It will be intelligent enough to precache or prebuild databases before being queried. Such an intelligent tool will be able to build whatever the most suited foundations are according to the wealth of the repository of queries and transformations throughout the history of BI.

The following checklist summarizes some of the key questions you should ask yourselves when designing data architecture for your BI projects:

Scoring: Not sure = 1 point, Basic understanding = 2 points, Clear understanding = 3 points

	Score
☐ What kind of dashboard(s) am I building?	
☐ What replication time requirements do I have? Real time? Daily? Weekly? Monthly?	
☐ Where is/are my data source(s)?	
☐ Where is my ODS? Do I need to build one?	
☐ Do I need to build an OLAP? What type will it be? Where will it be?	
☐ What technology is my Web portal based on? Java? .NET?	
☐ Do I possess, or have access to, expertise in database management systems?	
☐ Do I possess, or have access to, expertise in the necessary query languages?	
☐ What are the KPIs and the calculation definitions?	
☐ Do I possess, or have access to, expertise in the necessary dashboard tools?	
Total Score	

Place your total score in the right box in the following Scorecard:

Status	Points	Color	Your Score
Ready	21–30	🔵	
In Progress	15–20	⚪	
Not Ready	0–15	⚫	

PART 3

DASHBOARD DESIGN

T hus far, we have covered a great deal of general information about dashboards, such as their history and their importance to an organization. We have also covered the design process for metrics and key performance indicators (KPIs), the most essential components of a dashboard. Then we went on to describe various data architecture options to help facilitate and streamline the flow of data along with analytical options in dashboards. In this part we dive into the dashboard design itself. We will do so by first suggesting a formal process that can be used to guide dashboard design activities, next we will provide various layout tips, and finally we will provide many examples of completed dashboards.

Design Tips

14

f it is well planned and executed, the actual dashboard layout design process can be a very rewarding experience as the project team becomes exposed to key strategies, tactics, and processes. Quite often, the users will be very appreciative and excited about the outcome.

Effective business dashboards must be carefully designed with user roles and their responsibilities and decision timelines in mind. If the design process is carefully structured, chances of a successful project with long-term positive outcome for the organization will be very high. Furthermore, if a dashboard is successfully deployed in one part of the organization, the word is likely to spread quickly to other business units, and a well-structured design process and documentation can then be reused over and over again.

For an implementation team and other stakeholders in a dashboard project, nothing works better than having a well-organized approach to the project. A ten-step process for designing dashboards follows, which should provide a framework for your own design project. *Note:* Part 4 covers the actual project plans and provides in-depth material to help manage the project itself. The ten steps are as follows:

1. Come up with the implementation team (see Chapter 16).

2. Create a project plan (see Part 4).

3. Review the metrics and key performance indicators (KPIs) (see Chapter 5).

4. Prioritize the initial dashboards based on risk, chance for a quick win, and internal marketability.

5. Design the dashboard layout.

6. Clarify software, hardware, security, and architecture requirements (see Part 2 and Appendices A through D).

7. Obtain signoff from key stakeholders.

8. Build the dashboard (see Parts 2, 3, and 4).

9. Deploy the dashboard (see Parts 2 and 4).

10. Train the users (see Part 4).

Here in Part 3 we will focus on Step 5 (see the foregoing list) in the overall dashboard design process: design the dashboard layout. As was noted, the other steps are covered in other sections of the book.

Whereas creating the right metrics and data architecture is "mission critical" for long-term dashboard success, the visual presentation of the dashboard can be almost as important, because it will immediately send a message to users about quality and professionalism. In other words, a sloppy or chaotic screen design will get lower user adoption and less interest than a logical and easily readable dashboard, even if the information and functionality are exactly the same.

The following sections cover in detail all the key elements of dashboard design that you should plan for, including:

- Use of storyboards
- Components
- Use of color
- Layout and use of screen real estate
- Use of tables and scorecards
- Link to outside content (e.g., reports, articles, etc.)

CREATING A STORYBOARD

Let us first look at a recommended process for designing dashboard layouts. Having an organized approach to this activity will save time and effort in the overall project. We suggest that you use a method called "storyboarding" to arrive at your dashboard layouts.

Storyboards are graphic organizers, such as a series of illustrations or images displayed in sequence for the purpose of previsualizing a motion graphic or interactive media sequence, including website and computer interactivity. Storyboards are useful for preimplementation presentations to dashboard users and for ensuring that the steps of a process make sense.

The first known storyboards were used by the Walt Disney studios in the early 1930s, and now they are finding a good use in the design process for modern computerized dashboards. The benefit of storyboarding is to very quickly (within hours) be able to visualize what a dashboard will look like, without actually building it. A storyboard can be created with multiple mediums such as:

- Pen and paper
- Whiteboard
- PowerPoint
- Dashboard prototyping software

The main advantage of using a software solution for storyboarding is that dashboard designs can easily be copied and modified to make changes or to create additional dashboards. The ability to easily print out hard copies is another advantage.

STORYBOARD DESIGN PROCESS

Before we go into detailed design activities, here is a suggested seven-step storyboard process for design:

Step 1. Put together the storyboard team. The first step in this process is to gather the team that will create the storyboard. These are suggested team members:

- Project manager
- Data architect (knows how to design integrations, data warehouse, cubes)
- Data source expert (knows where the source data is located and how to access it—database connectors, name of database tables, etc.)
- Dashboard expert (knows capabilities of the dashboard software)
- Business unit manager (the main proponent and user of the dashboard who knows what he or she would like to see and analyze)
- Information technology (IT) manager (knows passwords, network logins, server names, etc.)

Some of the roles on the foregoing list might be filled by the same person.

Step 2. Gather all metrics. Chapter 5 covered metrics design in detail. To avoid "quick and dirty" ad hoc decisions on metrics, you should do the metrics design early on, as has been recommended in this book, and not during the middle of the dashboard layout project. In other words, you should have a list of metrics at this point and share them with the design team so that everyone knows what the drivers of the dashboard are.

Step 3. Gather all components available in the chosen dashboard technology. This activity consists of matching the metrics to the components that will display them in the dashboard. Based on the dashboard technology your organization has purchased, at this point your options are limited to what the chosen technology offers. Subsequently a number of popular components and recommendations for use will be presented.

Note: Before you proceed with this section, we suggest that you review all the examples in Chapter 15 and bring copies and ideas from the examples to the storyboard design team.

- Area Charts:
  - Area Chart—displays trends over time or categories (see Exhibit 14.1)
  - Stacked Area Chart—displays the trend of the contribution of each value over time or categories (see Exhibit 14.2)
  - 100% Stacked Area Chart—displays the trend of the percentage each value contributes over time or categories (see Exhibit 14.3)

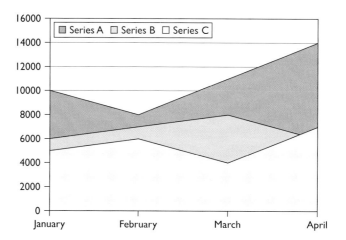

EXHIBIT 14.1 Area Chart

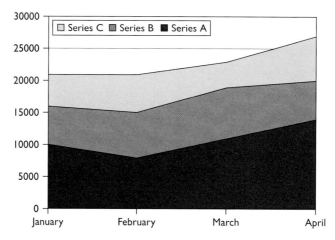

EXHIBIT 14.2 Area Chart, Stacked

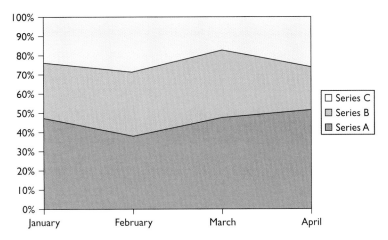

EXHIBIT 14.3 Area Chart, 100% Stacked

- Bar Charts:
  - Clustered Bar Chart—compares values across categories (see Exhibit 14.4)
  - Stacked Bar Chart—compares the contribution of each value to a total across categories (see Exhibit 14.5)
  - 100% Stacked Bar Chart—compares the percentage each value contributes to a value across categories (see Exhibit 14.6)
- Bubble Chart—compares three sets of values; similar to a Line Chart, but with a third value displayed as the size of the bubble marker (see Exhibit 14.7)
- Column Charts:
  - Clustered Column Chart—compares values across categories (see Exhibit 14.8)

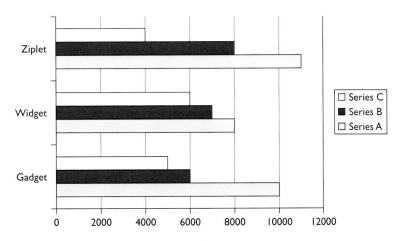

EXHIBIT 14.4 Bar Chart, Clustered

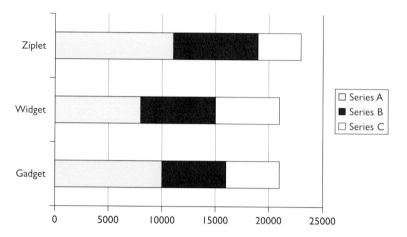

EXHIBIT 14.5 Bar Chart, Stacked

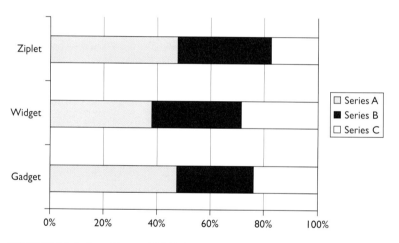

EXHIBIT 14.6 Bar Chart, 100% Stacked

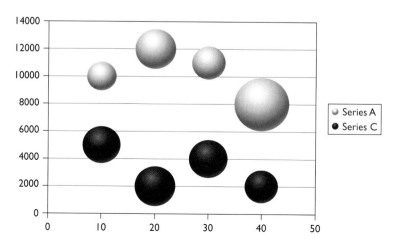

EXHIBIT 14.7 Bubble Chart

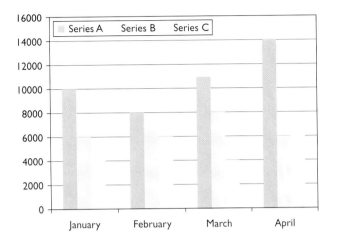

EXHIBIT 14.8 Column Chart, Clustered

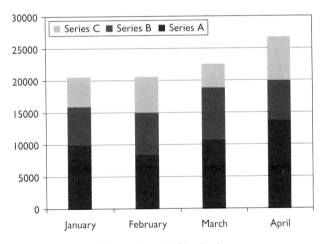

EXHIBIT 14.9 Column Chart, Stacked

- Stacked Column Chart—compares the contribution of each value to a total across categories (see Exhibit 14.9)
- 100% Stacked Column Chart—compares the percentage each value contributes to a value across categories (see Exhibit 14.10)
- Gauges—used to display a single value. Typically, a gauge will also use colors to indicate whether the value displayed is "good," "acceptable," or "bad" (see Exhibit 14.11)
- Grid Controls—used to present data in a grid or report format
- Icons—can be found in various shapes. Most popular are traffic lights (oval circles) or arrows used in conjunction with scorecards or reports to visualize and highlight variances. Colors like green,

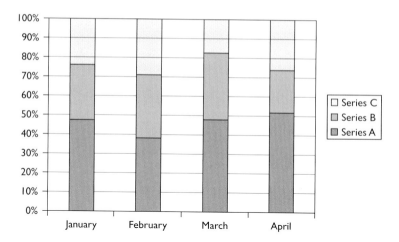

EXHIBIT 14.10 Column Chart, 100% Stacked

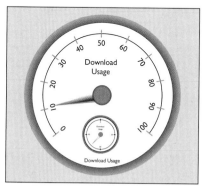

Cost (%) (vs. last month)

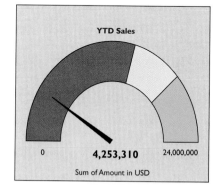

EXHIBIT 14.11 Gauges

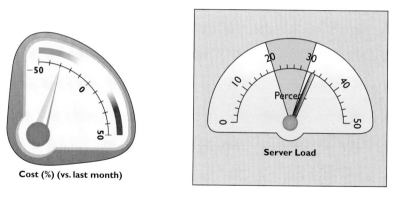

yellow, and red are used to indicate values as "good", "acceptable", or "bad" (see Exhibit 14.12)

▨ Images—most often images are used in a dashboard as logos or pictures of products, and so on

EXHIBIT 14.12 Icons

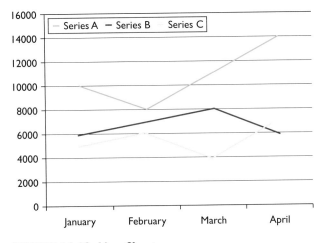

EXHIBIT 14.13 Line Chart

- Line Charts:
  - Line Chart—displays trends over time or categories (see Exhibit 14.13)
  - Stacked Line Chart—displays the trend of the contribution of each value over time or categories (see Exhibit 14.14)
  - 100% Stacked Line Chart—displays the trend of the percentage each value contributes over time or categories (see Exhibit 14.15)
- Pie Charts—display the contribution of each value to a total (see Exhibit 14.16)
- Other components. Vendors are continuously coming up with new dashboard objects to help designers present information to enhance monitoring and analysis. Make sure you do your own research to

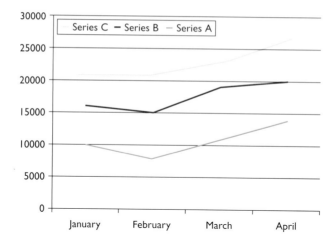

EXHIBIT 14.14 Line Chart, Stacked

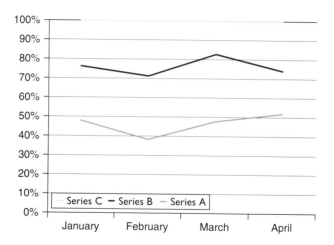

EXHIBIT 14.15 Line Chart, 100% Stacked

EXHIBIT 14.16 Pie Chart

see what is available for the platform and dashboard technology you are planning to use. Remember, the most fancy components are not always the best components. The rule of thumb is to choose dashboard components based on what most clearly presents the information to the user.

Step 4. Design dashboard layout. Once you have prepared all the metrics (step 2) and matched them to the chosen dashboard components (step 3), it is time to place them on the storyboard and come up with the layout on the screen.

Here are some rules of thumb to follow when you design the layout:

- *Colors.* You have a large number of colors to choose from, and although it is tempting to use a variety of different colors to highlight various areas of importance in a dashboard, most experts agree that too many colors and the "wrong" colors are worse than too few colors. Here are some tips:

  Note: Remember that some people are color blind, so if you use colors, try to use various shades. A good test is to print out a screenshot of the dashboard on a black and white printer and see whether you are able to distinguish what will now be shades of gray from each other.

- *Fonts and font size.* Using the right or wrong fonts and font sizes is like the use of colors; it can make or break the entire look and feel that a user gets from looking at a dashboard. Here are some tips:

  - Do not mix a number of different font types; try to stick with one. Use one of the popular business fonts, such as Arial.

  - Do not mix a number of different font sizes, and do not use too small or too large fonts. Remember that the dashboards likely will be used by many middle-aged or older employees who cannot easily read very small fonts. Ideally, you should use a font size of 12 or 14 points and apply boldface in headers (maybe with the exception of a main header that could be in a somewhat larger font). Text or numbers should be in fonts of 8 to 12 points, with 10 points being most often used. When it comes to font sizes, the challenge for a designer is always the available areas on the screen (also referred to as "screen real estate"). With overly large fonts, titles, legends, descriptions, and so on may get cut off or bleed into another section, and fonts that are too small make the display hard to read.

- *Use of screen real estate.* Per definition, most dashboards are designed to fit in a single viewable area (e.g., the user's computer screen) so users can easily get a view of all their key metrics by quickly glancing over the screen. In other words, the moment a "dashboard" is of a size that requires a lot of scrolling to the sides or up and down for users to find what they are looking for, it is not really a dashboard anymore, but a page with graphics. Almost always, users get excited about all the possibilities with a dashboard, and they want more charts and tables than what will easily fit on a screen. When this happens, there are various options:

- Use components that can be expanded, collapsed, or stacked so that the default views after login still fit on a single screen but users can click a button to expand out certain areas where they need to see more.

- Use many dashboards. If there is simply too much information to fit on a single dashboard, organize and categorize it and create several dashboards (e.g., move sales-related information to a "sales dashboard" and higher-level revenue and expense information to a "financial dashboard"). Many dashboard technologies have buttons or hyperlinks that let us link related dashboards together to make navigation easy and intuitive for the users.

- Use parameters to filter the data that the user wants to see. For example, a time parameter can display a specific quarter in a dashboard instead of showing all four quarters in a year.

- *Component placement.* If you have two tables or grids or scorecards and four charts, how should they be organized on the screen? Here are a few tips:

  - Talk with the key users to find out which information is most important so that you can establish a priority. Based on this, place the components in order of importance. Most users read from left to right and start at the top, so that could be the order you place the components. The idea is that if users have only a few seconds to glance at a dashboard, their eyes first catch what is most important to them.

  - A second consideration for component placement is workflow. In other words, if users typically start by analyzing metrics in a scorecard component and then want to see a graphical trend for a certain metric they click on in the scorecard, that chart component should be placed adjacent to the scorecard to make it easy for users to transfer their view to the chart as they click on the scorecard.

Step 5. Assign dashboard title and component labels. In the last few steps, you have designed the dashboard layout by selecting the components and carefully positioning them on the storyboard, and you chose the appropriate fonts, colors, and so on for the components. The next step is to create the dashboard title and component labels. In most software, component labels are a part of the properties for the individual components, although some solutions have free-standing labels you can place anywhere you want on the dashboard. Regardless, here are some general tips:

- Use fonts, font sizes, and colors that match what you did for all the components.
- Carefully select short, but clear and concise headers and labels. A confusing label can misguide users' analyses, because they may think they are looking at something different than what is actually displayed. Therefore, even though headers and labels are very easy to set up, do not rush this stage of the design process.

Step 6. Specify core dashboard functionality (filters, drill down, alerts, etc.). Most dashboard technologies offer various types of filters ("drop-downs") whereby a user can select dimensions such as department, roll-up levels, time period, and so on. These selections will then filter the related data for either the entire dashboard (i.e., a global filter was used) or for one or more component in the dashboard. This is an important issue you should discuss with the users so they get to choose the data they want to see as well as which components should be affected by the choices they make in the filters.

Step 7. Present the dashboard *prototype to the users for possible adjustments and approval.* Once the storyboard has been completed, set up a demonstration for the key users. The outcome should be an approval and sign-off on each dashboard you storyboarded. If there are comments leading to changes, take careful notes or (if feasible) make the changes directly in the storyboard while the users are present and then get sign-off.

The sign-off is important, as the storyboard will typically drive a number of decisions made by the architecture and dashboard design team(s) and will affect many of the hours they will spend. You do not want to be in a situation where at the end of a project you present a dashboard that does not correspond to users' requirements.

Dashboard Examples

15

I n chapter 14, we covered the dashboard design process and offered tips to optimize layout and use of components. In this chapter we will cover a large number of dashboard examples, organized by three main categories—strategic dashboards, tactical dashboards, and operational dashboards.

The examples provided in this chapter include real-life dashboards and designs graciously provided by various software vendors and consulting companies. It is suggested that you use these examples to find ideas for your own dashboard project. In some cases, you may find the dashboards useful in their entirety, while in other cases, they may provide you with ideas for use of different components, colors, fonts, metrics, screen layout, and so on. You should review these examples prior to starting on Step 3 in the dashboard design process covered in Chapter 14.

In order for you to easily interpret and find the dashboards of interest, each dashboard example is categorized the following way:

- Dashboard category
- Industry (retail, services, manufacturing, education, public sector, etc.)
- Functional area (sales, finance, human resources, operations, executive, etc.)

Many dashboards and metrics are often similar across industries, so make sure you take the time to browse all the examples: you may find valuable ideas in any of the images provided.

OVERVIEW: DASHBOARD EXAMPLES

The following table contains a comprehensive list of all the dashboard examples in this chapter. It is designed to help you quickly find the examples that may be of most interest to you.

Dashboard category	Industry	Exhibit Number	Function or Organization Level
Strategic	Education	15.1	Executive
Strategic	Non-Specific	15.2	Executive
Strategic	Public Sector	15.3	Executive
Strategic	Public Sector	15.4	Executive
Strategic	Manufacturing	15.5	Executive
Strategic	Non-Specific	15.6	HR
Strategic	Education	15.7	Executive
Strategic	Public Sector	15.8	Executive
Strategic	Non-Specific	15.9	Executive
Strategic	Non-Specific	15.10	Executive
Strategic	Non-Specific	15.11	Executive
Strategic	Non-Specific	15.12	Executive
Strategic	Manufacturing	15.13	Divisional
Strategic	Manufacturing	15.14	Executive
Strategic	Manufacturing	15.15	Divisional
Strategic	Healthcare	15.16	Executive
Strategic	Manufacturing	15.17	Sales
Strategic	Non-Specific	15.18	Operations
Strategic	Financial (bank)	15.19	Finance
Strategic	Financial (bank)	15.20	Finance
Strategic	Pharmaceutical	15.21	Executive
Tactical	Public Sector	15.22	Customer Service

Tactical	Manufacturing	15.23	Executive
Tactical	Manufacturing	15.24	Sales
Tactical	Public Sector	15.25	Revenue
Tactical	Public Sector	15.26	Revenue (taxes)
Tactical	Non-Specific	15.27	Divisional
Tactical	Manufacturing	15.28	Executive
Tactical	Non-Specific	15.29	Sales
Tactical	Non-Specific	15.30	Sales
Tactical	Non-Specific	15.31	Sales
Tactical	Non-Specific	15.32	Sales
Tactical	Retail	15.33	Sales
Tactical	Retail	15.34	Sales
Tactical	Retail	15.35	Sales
Tactical	Non-Specific	15.36	Sales (CRM)
Tactical	Non-Specific	15.37	Budget
Tactical	Non-Specific	15.38	Finance
Tactical	Non-Specific	15.39	Finance
Tactical	Non-Specific	15.40	Finance
Tactical	Non-Specific	15.41	Finance
Tactical	Manufacturing	15.42	Finance
Tactical	Manufacturing	15.43	Operation
Tactical	Non-Specific	15.44	Human Resources
Tactical	Non-Specific	15.45	Information Technology
Tactical	Public Sector	15.46	Financal Services
Tactical	Public Sector	15.47	Financial
Tactical	Public Sector	15.48	Finance
Tactical	Public Sector	15.49	Budget
Tactical	Public Sector	15.50	Customer Service

(Continued)

Dashboard category	Industry	Exhibit Number	Function or Organization Level
Tactical	Education	15.51	Academic
Tactical	Education	15.52	Academic
Tactical	Education	15.53	Finance
Tactical	Education	15.54	Admissions
Tactical	Education	15.55	Finance
Tactical	Education	15.56	Recruiting
Tactical	Education	15.57	Enrollment
Tactical	Financial (bank)	15.58	Executive
Tactical	Energy (oil and gas)	15.59	Executive
Tactical	Manufacturing	15.60	Production
Operational	Transportation	15.61	Executive
Operational	Non-Specific	15.62	Sales (CRM)
Operational	Real Estate	15.63	Sales
Operational	Non-Specific	15.64	Sales (CRM)
Operational	Non-Specific	15.65	Sales
Operational	Non-Specific	15.66	Sales (CRM)
Operational	Non-Specific	15.67	Sales (CRM)
Operational	Retail	15.68	Sales
Operational	Non-Specific	15.69	Marketing (online)
Operational	Non-Specific	15.70	Marketing (online)
Operational	Non-Specific	15.71	Marketing (online)
Operational	Non-Specific	15.72	Marketing (online)
Operational	Financial Services (bank)	15.73	Finance
Operational	Non-Specific	15.74	Finance
Operational	Non-Specific	15.75	Finance
Operational	Non-Specific	15.76	Finance

Operational	Non-Specific	15.77	Finance
Operational	Manufacturing	15.78	Operations
Operational	Manufacturing	15.79	Operations
Operational	Non-Specific	15.80	Human Resources
Operational	Non-Specific	15.81	Information Technology
Operational	Non-Specific	15.82	Customer Service
Operational	Non-Specific	15.83	Customer Service
Operational	Education	15.84	Student Relations
Operational	Healthcare	15.85	Hospital (Patient care)
Operational	Transportation	15.86	Operations
Operational	Hospitality	15.87	Operations
Operational	Non-Specific	15.88	Mobile
Operational	Non-Specific	15.89	Mobile
Operational	Non-Specific	15.90	Operation
Operational	Public Sector	15.91	Customer Service
Operational	Public Sector	15.92	Healthcare
Operational	Education	15.93	Finance
Operational	Education (K–12)	15.94	Academic
Operational	Financial (bank)	15.95	Executive
Operational	Energy (oil and gas)	15.96	Operations
Operational	Pharmaceutical	15.97	Financial
Operational	Non-Specific	15.98	Project Management
Operational	Non-Specific	15.99	Project Management
Operational	Non-Specific	15.100	Project Management
Operational	Non-Specific	15.101	Project Management

(Continued)

Dashboard category	Industry	Exhibit Number	Function or Organization Level
Operational	Education (K–12)	15.102	Administration (curriculum)
Operational	Education (K–12)	15.103	Administration (school level)
Operational	Education (K–12)	15.104	Principal (Campus level)
Operational	Education (K–12)	15.105	Teacher (class level)
Operational	Non-Specific	15.106	Operations
Operational	Non-Specific	15.107	IT
Operational	Non-Specific	15.108	Finance
Operational	Retail	15.109	Sales
Operational	Non-Specific	15.110	Finance
Operational	Non-Specific	15.111	Finance
Operational	Non-Specific	15.112	Sales (CRM)
Operational	Non-Specific	15.113	Finance

STRATEGIC DASHBOARDS

As discussed in an early part of this book, an organization would use strategic dashboards to monitor progress toward strategic objectives. An executive-level dashboard might reflect enterprise-wide strategic goals and corresponding key performance indicators (KPIs). Enterprise-wide strategic dashboards often "cascade" down to the department level, while retaining alignment to the corporate objectives.

Users of strategic dashboards are the managers in the organization who are involved with strategy execution and related monitoring of progress.

TACTICAL DASHBOARDS

Organizations use tactical dashboards to monitor progress and related trends for each of their strategic initiatives. This can include key projects, and both initiatives and projects are often measured against a preset goal (e.g., a budget or a target). Because tactical dashboards can be quite focused, they are ideally deployed with a technology that allows for drill down to detail and "slicing and dicing" the data—for example, to analyze why certain targets have not been met and where the problem is occurring.

Users of tactical dashboards are the managers involved with the individual tactical activities that are deployed to support the organization's strategies.

OPERATIONAL DASHBOARDS

As discussed earlier in the book, dashboards in this category are used to monitor business processes, business activities, and complex events. Usually the display will provide daily updates or near real-time charts and reports that indicate the status of business or manufacturing processes. Because managers use the dashboards frequently, they can discover issues and take action to fix problems or take advantage of opportunities. Because of the practical nature of operational dashboards, they are most typically used at the departmental level (where "operations take place") and not at the top executive level. The latter user would typically use a tactical or strategic dashboard to monitor just a point-in-time aggregate metric or two from each operational dashboard.

Users of operational dashboards have a narrow scope of responsibility (sales, help desk services, etc.) that dictates the need for more detailed information with strong analytical functionality to perform root-cause analysis on the displayed data.

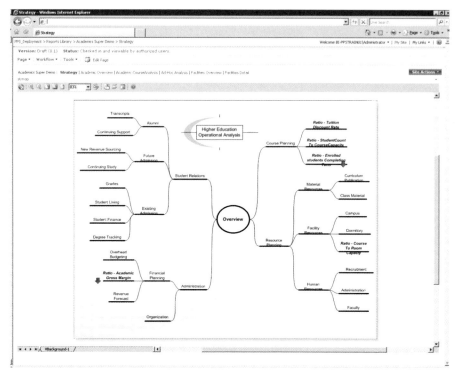

**EXHIBIT 15.1 Category: Strategic Dashboard; Industry: Education;
Functional/Organizational Level: Executive**

Source: Printed with permission—Solver, Inc. (www.solverusa.com).

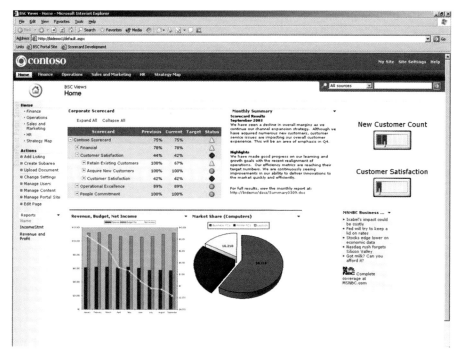

**EXHIBIT 15.2 Category: Strategic Dashboard; Industry: Nonspecific;
Functional/Organizational Level: Executive**

Source: Reprinted with permission from Microsoft Corporation.

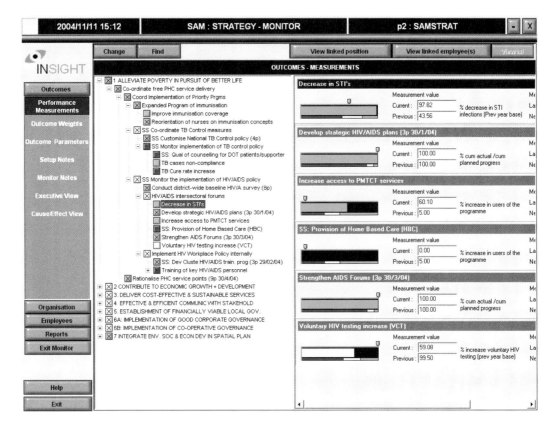

EXHIBIT 15.3 Category: Strategic Dashboard; Industry: Public Sector; Functional/ Organizational Level: Executive

Source: Copyright: Furno Investments No 1 Pty Ltd., Republic of South Africa. Credit: Furno Investment No 1 Pty Ltd., Republic of South Africa, PO Box 14363, Lyttleton 0140, South Africa.

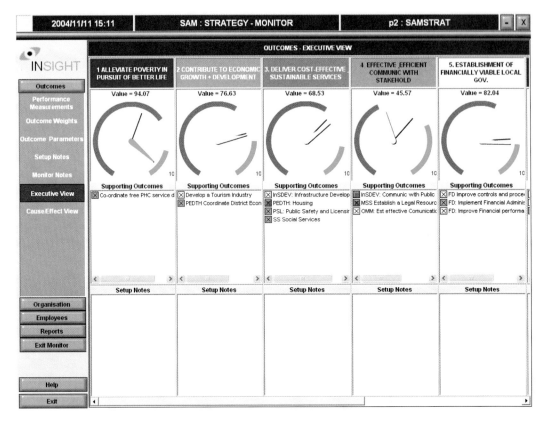

EXHIBIT 15.4 Category: Strategic Dashboard; Industry: Public Sector; Functional/ Organizational Level: Executive

Source: Copyright: Furno Investments No 1 Pty Ltd., Republic of South Africa. Credit: Furno Investment No 1 Pty Ltd., Republic of South Africa, PO Box 14363, Lyttleton 0140, South Africa.

Strategic Dashboard

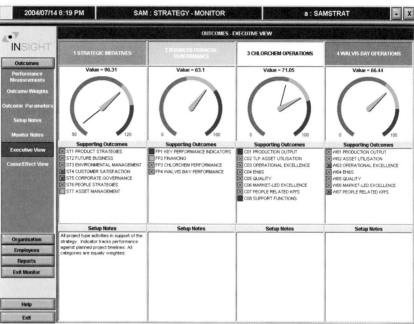

EXHIBIT 15.5 Category: Strategic Dashboard; Industry: Manufacturing; Functional/Organizational Level: Executive

Source: Copyright: Furno Investments No 1 Pty Ltd., Republic of South Africa. Credit: Furno Investment No 1 Pty Ltd., Republic of South Africa, PO Box 14363, Lyttleton 0140, South Africa.

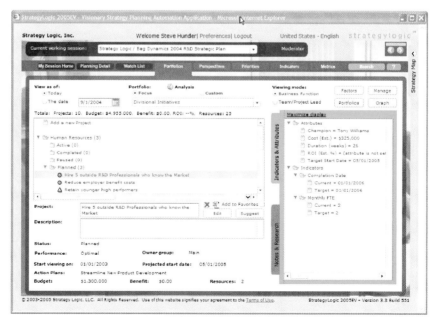

EXHIBIT 15.6 Category: Strategic Dashboard; Industry: Nonspecific; Functional/Organizational Level: Human Resources

Source: Used with permission, Strategy Logic LLC.

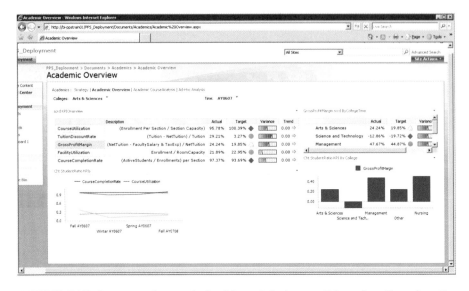

EXHIBIT 15.7 Category: Strategic Dashboard; Industry: Education; Functional/Organizational Level: Executive

Source: Printed with permission—Solver, Inc. (www.solverusa.com).

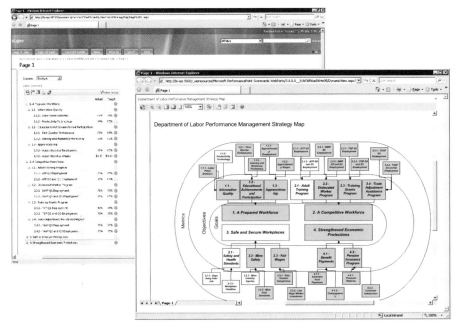

EXHIBIT 15.8 Category: Strategic Dashboard; Industry: Public Sector; Functional/Organizational Level: Executive

Source: Reprinted with permission from Microsoft Corporation.

EXHIBIT 15.9 Category: Strategic Dashboard; Industry: Nonspecific; Functional/ Organizational Level: Executive

Source: Reprinted with permission from Microsoft Corporation.

EXHIBIT 15.10 Category: Strategic Dashboard; Industry: Nonspecific; Functional/ Organizational Level: Executive

Source: Reprinted with permission from Microsoft Corporation.

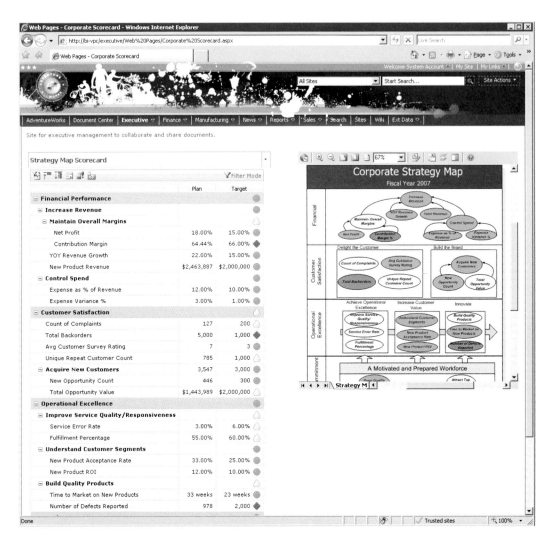

EXHIBIT 15.11 Category: Strategic Dashboard; Industry: Nonspecific; Functional/Organizational Level: Executive

Source: Reprinted with permission from Microsoft Corporation.

EXHIBIT 15.12 Category: Strategic Dashboard; Industry: Nonspecific; Functional/Organizational Level: Executive

Source: Reprinted with permission from Microsoft Corporation.

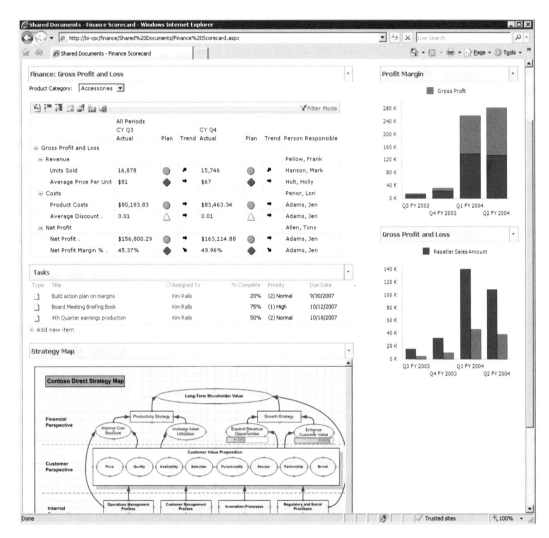

EXHIBIT 15.13 **Category: Strategic Dashboard; Industry: Manufacturing; Functional/Organizational Level: Divisional**

Source: Reprinted with permission from Microsoft Corporation.

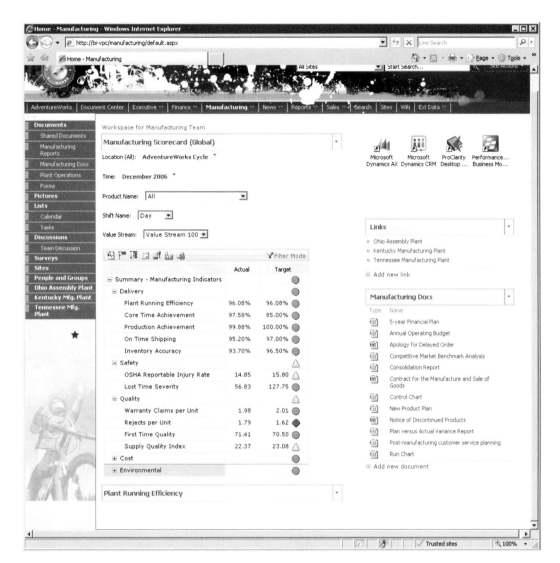

EXHIBIT 15.14 Category: Strategic Dashboard; Industry: Manufacturing; Functional/ Organizational Level: Executive

Source: Reprinted with permission from Microsoft Corporation.

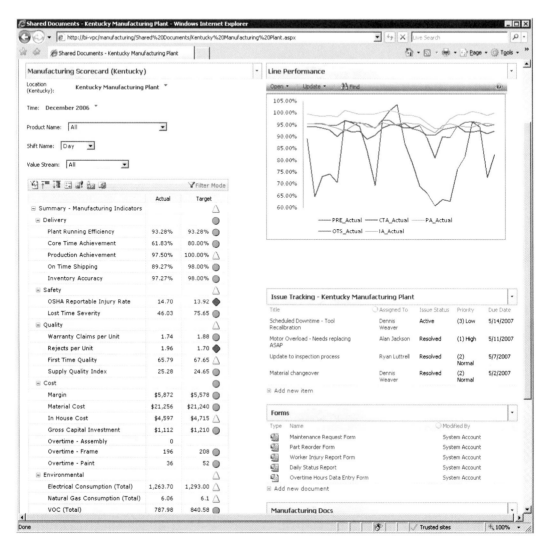

EXHIBIT 15.15 Category: Strategic Dashboard; Industry: Manufacturing; Functional/ Organizational Level: Divisional

Source: Reprinted with permission from Microsoft Corporation.

EXHIBIT 15.16 Category: Strategic Dashboard; Industry: Healthcare; Functional/ Organizational Level: Executive

Source: Reprinted with permission from Microsoft Corporation.

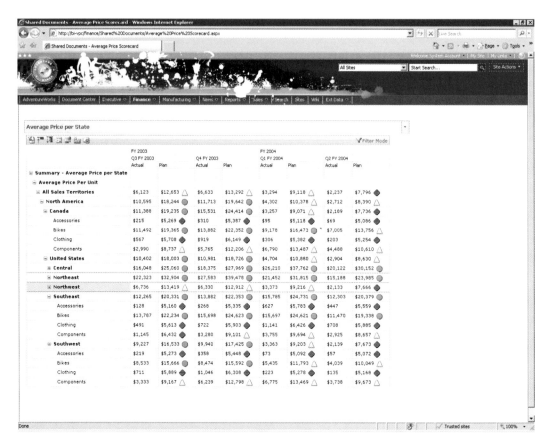

**EXHIBIT 15.17 Category: Strategic Dashboard; Industry: Manufacturing; Functional/
Organizational Level: Sales**

Source: Reprinted with permission from Microsoft Corporation.

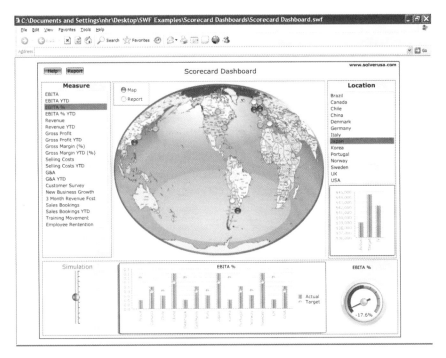

EXHIBIT 15.18 Category: Strategic Dashboard; Industry: Nonspecific; Functional/Organizational Level: Operations

Source: Printed with permission—Solver, Inc. (www.solverusa.com).

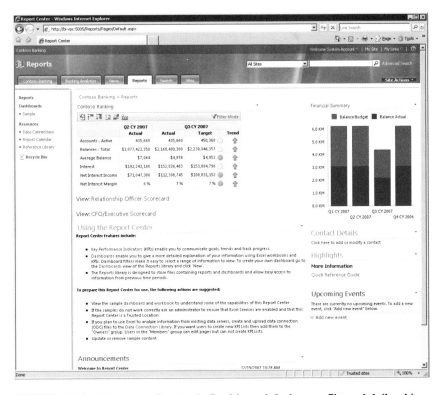

EXHIBIT 15.19 Category: Strategic Dashboard; Industry: Financial (bank); Functional/Organizational Level: Finance

Source: Reprinted with permission from Microsoft Corporation.

EXHIBIT 15.20 Category: Strategic Dashboard; Industry: Financial (bank); Functional/Organizational Level: Finance

Source: Reprinted with permission from Microsoft Corporation.

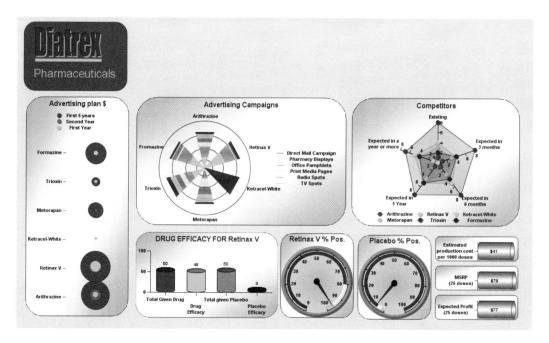

EXHIBIT 15.21 Category: Strategic Dashboard; Industry: Pharmaceutical; Functional/ Organizational Level: Executive

Source: This Visual Mining NetCharts Software product screenshot reprinted with permission of Visual Mining, Inc. © 2007 Visual Mining. All Rights Reserved.

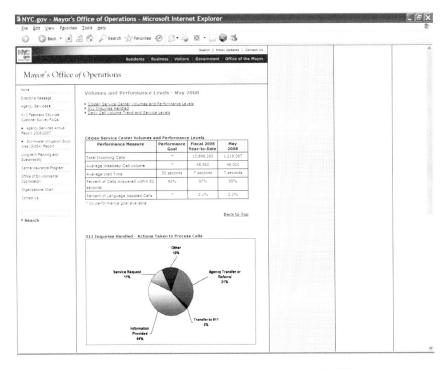

EXHIBIT 15.22 Category: Tactical Dashboard; Industry: Public Sector; Functional/Organizational Level: Customer Service
Source: Used with the permission of the City of New York. ©2008 New York City Department of Information Technology and Telecommunications. All Rights Reserved.

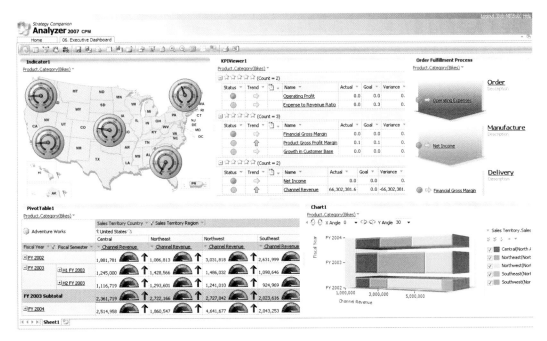

EXHIBIT 15.23 Category: Tactical Dashboard; Industry: Manufacturing; Functional/Organizational Level: Executive
Source: Reprinted with permission from Strategy Companion.

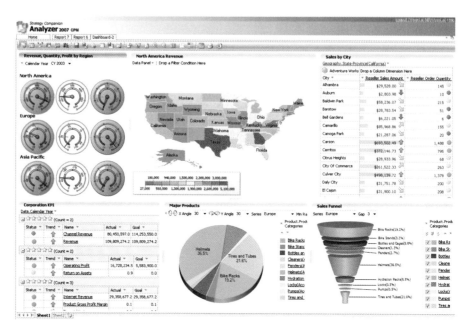

EXHIBIT 15.24 Category: Tactical Dashboard; Industry: Manufacturing; Functional/Organizational Level: Sales

Source: Reprinted with permission from Strategy Companion.

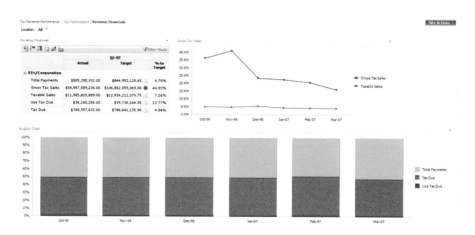

EXHIBIT 15.25 Category: Tactical Dashboard; Industry: Public Sector; Functional/Organizational Level: Revenue (taxes)

Source: Reprinted with permission from Microsoft Corporation.

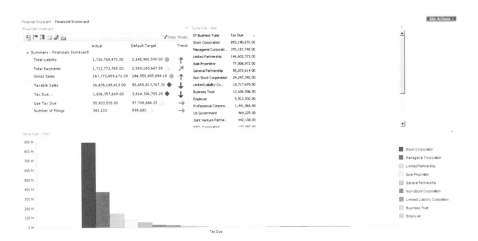

EXHIBIT 15.26 Category: Tactical Dashboard; Industry: Public Sector; Functional/Organizational Level: Revenue (taxes)

Source: Reprinted with permission from Microsoft Corporation.

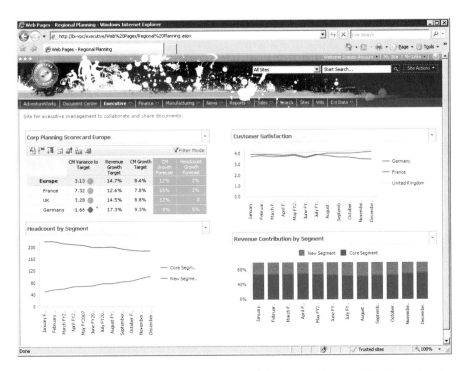

EXHIBIT 15.27 Category: Tactical Dashboard; Industry: Nonspecific; Functional/Organizational Level: Divisional

Source: Reprinted with permission from Microsoft Corporation.

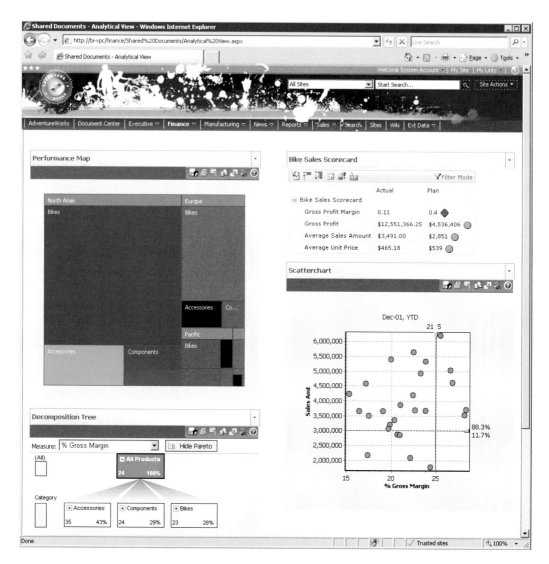

EXHIBIT 15.28 Category: Tactical Dashboard; Industry: Manufacturing; Functional/Organizational Level: Executive

Source: Reprinted with permission from Microsoft Corporation.

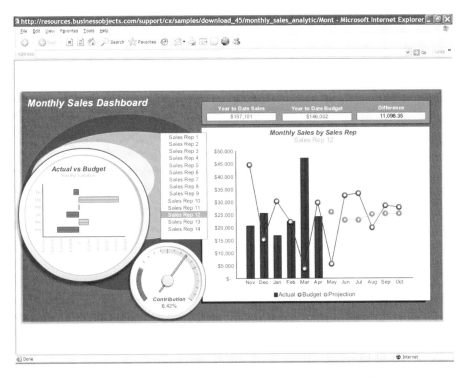

EXHIBIT 15.29 Category: Tactical Dashboard; Industry: Nonspecific; Functional/Organizational Level: Sales

Source: Used with permission of Business Objects Americas.

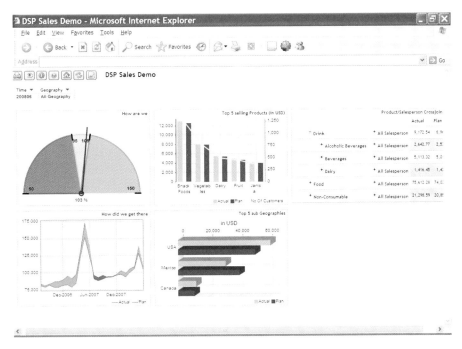

EXHIBIT 15.30 Category: Tactical Dashboard; Industry: Nonspecific; Functional/ Organizational Level: Sales

Source: Used with permission of DS Panel.

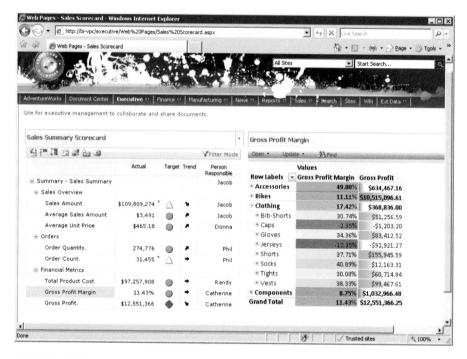

**EXHIBIT 15.31 Category: Tactical Dashboard; Industry: Nonspecific; Functional/
Organizational Level: Sales**

Source: Reprinted with permission from Microsoft Corporation.

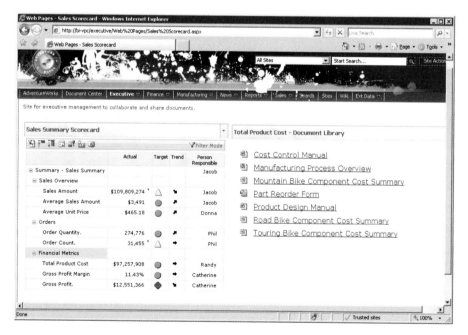

**EXHIBIT 15.32 Category: Tactical Dashboard; Industry: Nonspecific; Functional/
Organizational Level: Sales**

Source: Reprinted with permission from Microsoft Corporation.

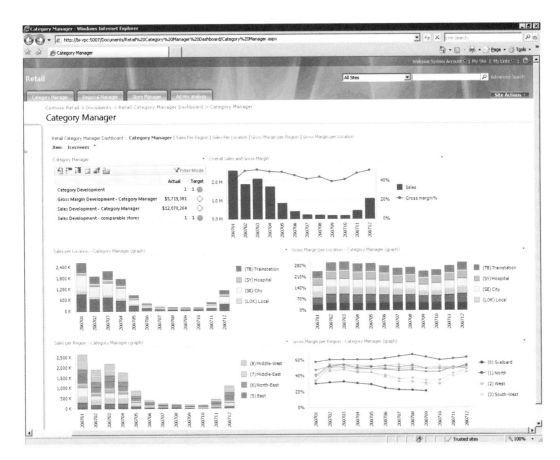

EXHIBIT 15.33 Category: Tactical Dashboard; Industry: Retail; Functional/Organizational Level: Sales

Source: Reprinted with permission from Microsoft Corporation.

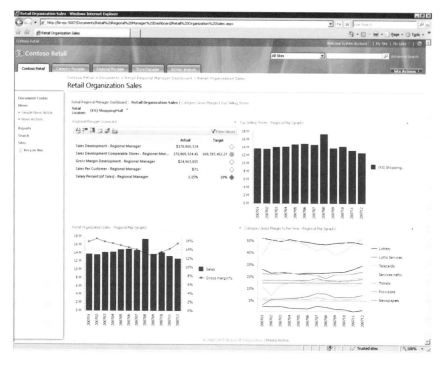

EXHIBIT 15.34 Category: Tactical Dashboard; Industry: Retail; Functional/ Organizational Level: Sales

Source: Reprinted with permission from Microsoft Corporation.

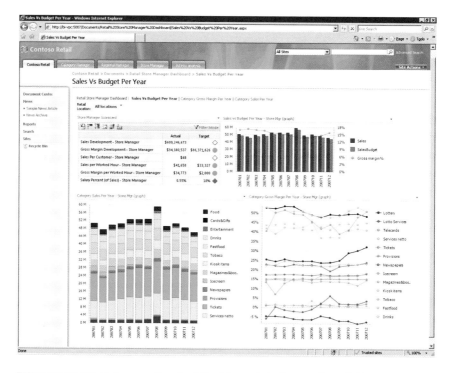

EXHIBIT 15.35 Category: Tactical Dashboard; Industry: Retail; Functional/ Organizational Level: Sales

Source: Reprinted with permission from Microsoft Corporation.

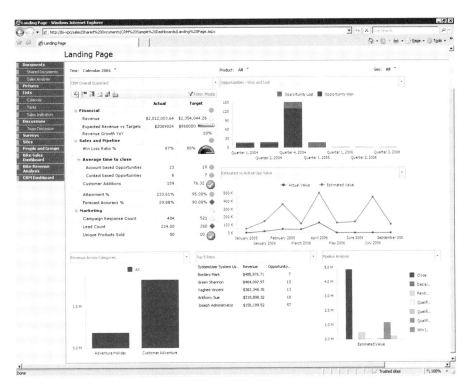

**EXHIBIT 15.36 Category: Tactical Dashboard; Industry: Nonspecific; Functional/
Organizational Level: Sales (CRM)**

Source: Reprinted with permission from Microsoft Corporation.

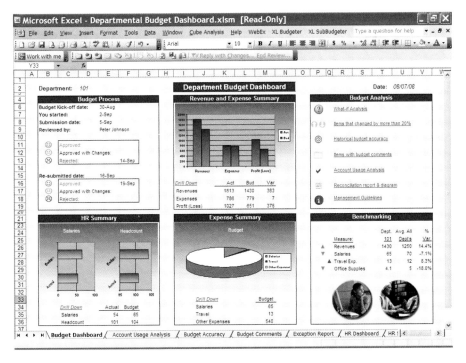

**EXHIBIT 15.37 Category: Tactical Dashboard; Industry: Nonspecific; Functional/
Organizational Level: Budget**

Source: Printed with permission—Solver, Inc. (www.solverusa.com).

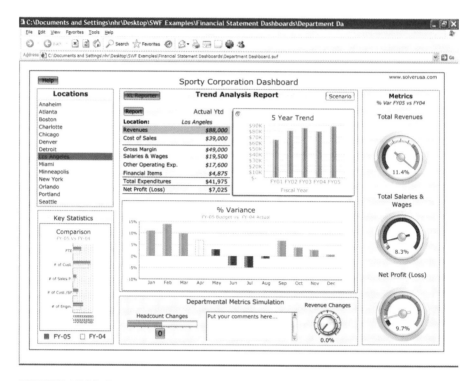

EXHIBIT 15.38 Category: Tactical Dashboard; Industry: Nonspecific; Functional/Organizational Level: Finance

Source: Printed with permission—Solver, Inc. (www.solverusa.com).

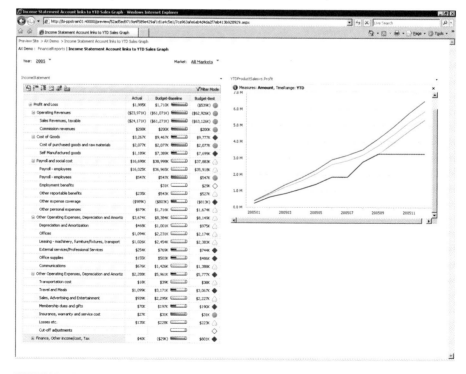

EXHIBIT 15.39 Category: Tactical Dashboard; Industry: Nonspecific; Functional/Organizational Level: Finance

Source: Printed with permission—Solver, Inc. (www.solverusa.com).

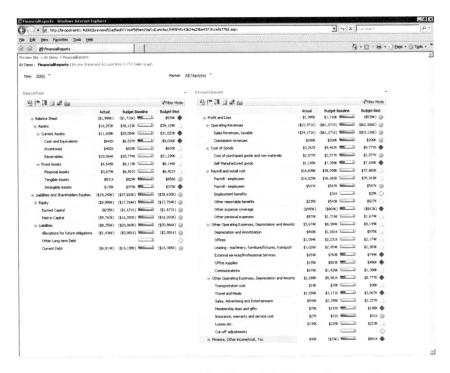

EXHIBIT 15.40 Category: Tactical Dashboard; Industry: Nonspecific; Functional/Organizational Level: Finance

Source: Printed with permission—Solver, Inc. (www.solverusa.com).

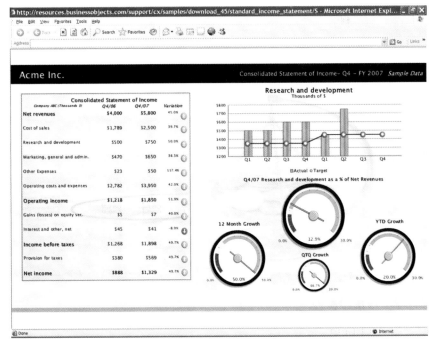

EXHIBIT 15.41 Category: Tactical Dashboard; Industry: Nonspecific; Functional/Organizational Level: Finance

Source: Used with permission of Business Objects Americas.

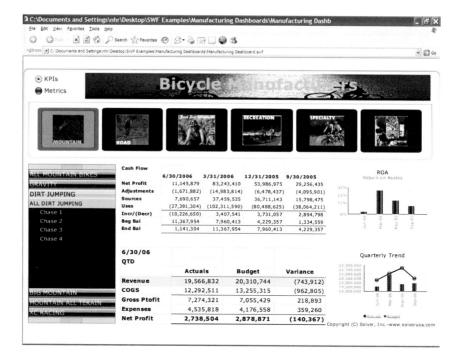

EXHIBIT 15.42 Category: Tactical Dashboard; Industry: Manufacturing; Functional/Organizational Level: Finance

Source: Printed with permission—Solver, Inc. (www.solverusa.com).

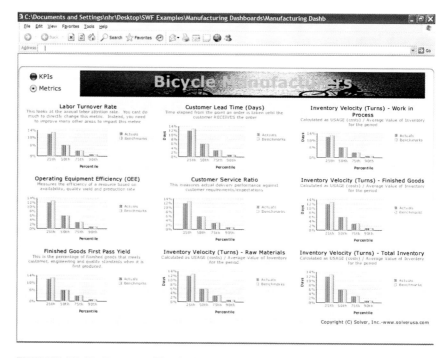

EXHIBIT 15.43 Category: Tactical Dashboard; Industry: Manufacturing; Functional/Organizational Level: Operations

Source: Printed with permission—Solver, Inc. (www.solverusa.com).

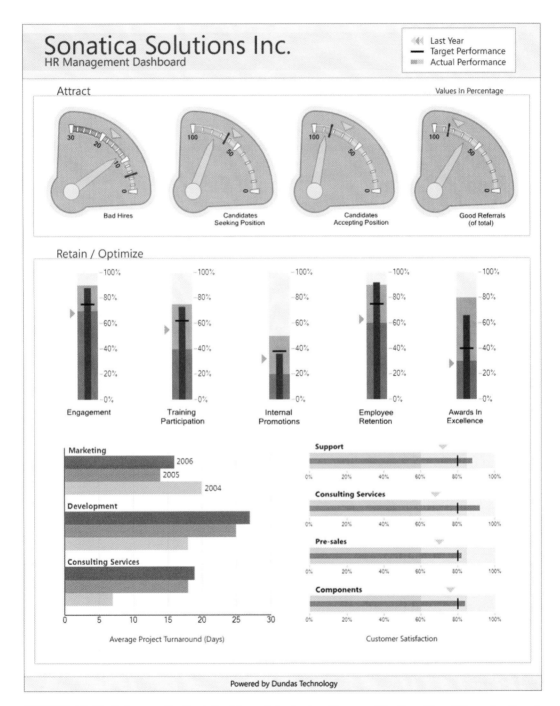

EXHIBIT 15.44 Category: Tactical Dashboard; Industry: Nonspecific; Functional/Organizational Level: Human Resources

Source: Dashboard provided courtesy of Dundas Data Visualization—www.dundas.com.

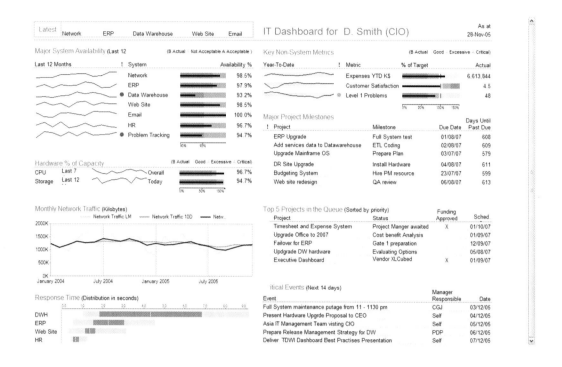

EXHIBIT 15.45 Category: Tactical Dashboard; Industry: Nonspecific; Functional/Organizational Level: Information Technology

Source: Dashboard implemented using XLCubed's MicroCharts, from the original design by Stephen Few.

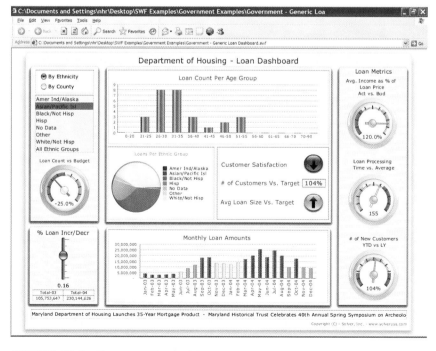

EXHIBIT 15.46 Category: Tactical Dashboard; Industry: Public Sector; Functional/Organizational Level: Financial Services

Source: Printed with permission—Solver, Inc. (www.solverusa.com.

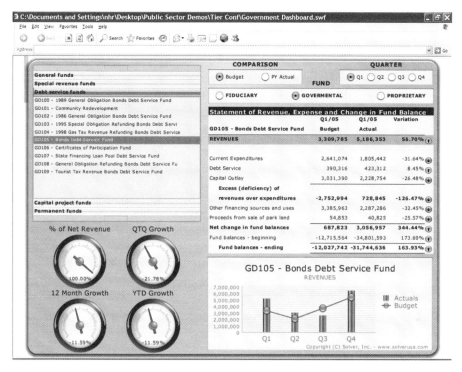

EXHIBIT 15.47 Category: Tactical Dashboard; Industry: Public Sector; Functional/Organizational Level: Financial

Source: Printed with permission—Solver, Inc. (www.solverusa.com).

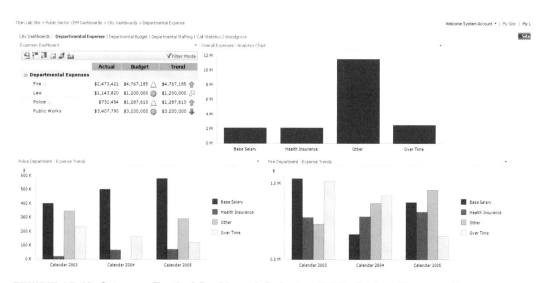

EXHIBIT 15.48 Category: Tactical Dashboard; Industry: Public Sector; Functional/ Organizational Level: Finance

Source: Reprinted with permission from Microsoft Corporation.

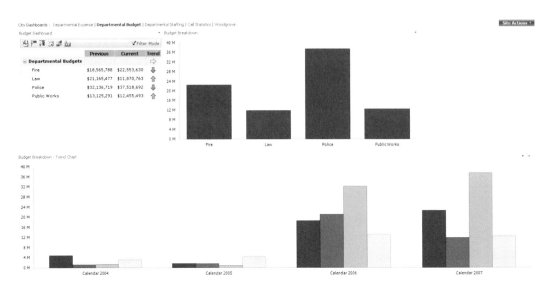

EXHIBIT 15.49 **Category: Tactical Dashboard; Industry: Public Sector; Functional/ Organizational Level: Budget**

Source: Reprinted with permission from Microsoft Corporation.

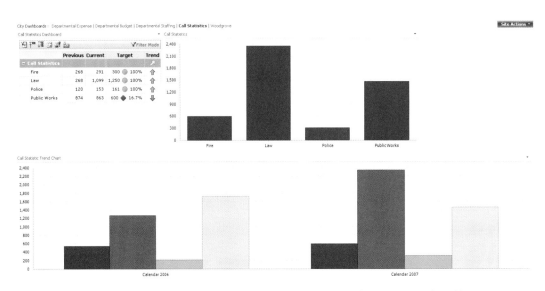

EXHIBIT 15.50 **Category: Tactical Dashboard; Industry: Public Sector; Functional/ Organizational Level: Customer Service**

Source: Reprinted with permission from Microsoft Corporation.

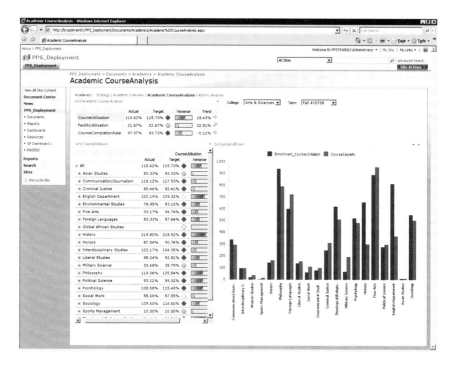

EXHIBIT 15.51 Category: Tactical Dashboard; Industry: Education; Functional/Organizational Level: Academic

Source: Printed with permission—Solver, Inc. (www.solverusa.com).

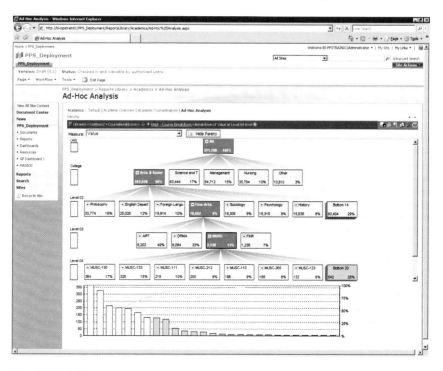

EXHIBIT 15.52 Category: Tactical Dashboard; Industry: Education; Functional/Organizational Level: Academic

Source: Printed with permission—Solver, Inc. (www.solverusa.com).

Financials

University Financial Analysis : Financials | YID and X2 Pivot

Collage: School of Management *   Year: AY0607 *

Financial ScoreCard   IncomeBy Dept

	Actual	Budget		
			3 ● 17	⟲ Filter Mode
⊟ Amount				
⊟ All	-9,494,763	-9,447,024	● 100.5%	
⊟ Revenue	7,804,608	7,410,057	○ 105.3%	
Allowances	149,972	142,390	○ 105.3%	
Gifts, Grants & Contracts	1,363,413	1,294,488	○ 105.3%	
Parking	683,373	648,826	○ 105.3%	
Reimbursements	46,959	44,585	○ 105.3%	
Sales & Services	275,949	261,999	○ 105.3%	
Student Fees	4,241,135	4,026,730	○ 105.3%	
Total Return	1,043,806	991,038	○ 105.3%	
⊟ Expense	17,299,390	16,657,000	○ 102.6%	
Capitalized Purchases	179,967	170,869	○ 105.3%	
Other Expenses	18,337	17,410	○ 105.3%	
Other	519,103	492,061	○ 105.3%	
Planning & Construction	78,785	74,803	○ 105.3%	
Professional Service Fees	213,347	202,562	○ 105.3%	
Salary	12,834,910	12,618,295	○ 101.7%	
Scholarship, Fellowship & Match	317,941	301,868	○ 105.3%	
Supplies & Services	1,033,453	981,209	○ 105.3%	
Travel	1,346,525	1,278,454	○ 105.3%	
Utilities	757,022	718,752	○ 105.3%	

	Actual	Budget		
			1 ◇ 13 ● 1	⟲ Filter Mode
⊟ Amount				
⊟ Academic Programs			◇ 0%	
ENT			◇ 0%	
FIN			◇ 0%	
MKT			◇ 0%	
⊟ Fin. & Admin.	13,970,795	13,593,914	● 102.8%	
Accounting	4,142,092	3,959,105	● 104.7%	
Human Resources	168,251	159,744	● 105.3%	
⊟ Enrollment Management	9,660,452	9,478,063	● 101.9%	
Financial Aid	24,000	24,000	● 100%	
Student Development	676,267	657,734	● 102.4%	
Academic Affairs	3,094,834	3,010,930	● 102.8%	
Instruction	4,066,246	4,044,015	● 100.5%	
Registration	1,799,105	1,741,363	● 100.3%	
⊟ IT Services	1,706,333	1,657,770	● 102.9%	
Information Technology Services	1,706,333	1,657,770	● 102.9%	
Office of the President	1,028,891	1,012,026	● 101.7%	
⊟ Operations, Planning and Construction	593,371	593,371	● 100%	
Engineering	593,371	593,371	● 100%	

EXHIBIT 15.53 Category: Tactical Dashboard; Industry: Education; Functional/ Organizational Level: Finance

Source: Printed with permission—Solver, Inc. (www.solverusa.com).

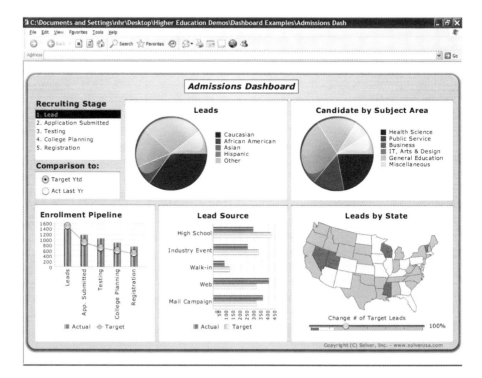

EXHIBIT 15.54 Category: Tactical Dashboard; Industry: Education; Functional/ Organizational Level: Admissions

Source: Printed with permission—Solver, Inc. (www.solverusa.com).

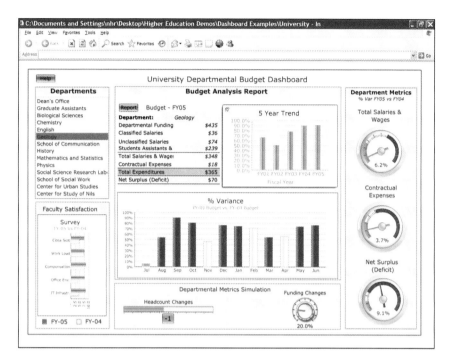

EXHIBIT 15.55 Category: Tactical Dashboard; Industry: Education; Functional/Organizational Level: Finance

Source: Printed with permission—Solver, Inc. (www.solverusa.com).

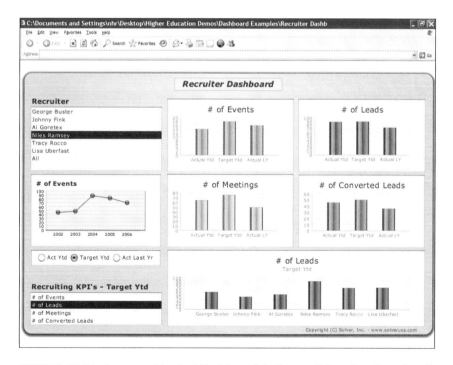

EXHIBIT 15.56 Category: Tactical Dashboard; Industry: Education; Functional/ Organizational Level: Recruiting

Source: Printed with permission—Solver, Inc. (www.solverusa.com).

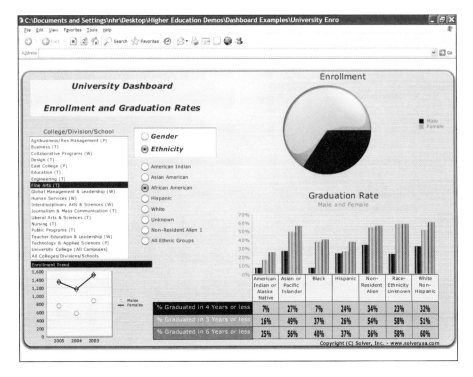

EXHIBIT 15.57 Category: Tactical Dashboard; Industry: Education; Functional/ Organizational Level: Enrollment

Source: Printed with permission—Solver, Inc. (www.solverusa.com).

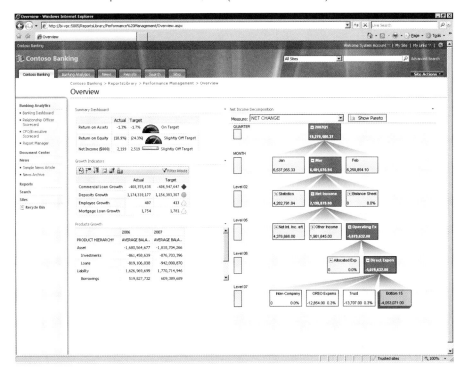

EXHIBIT 15.58 Category: Tactical Dashboard; Industry: Financial (bank); Functional/Organizational Level: Executive

Source: Reprinted with permission from Microsoft Corporation.

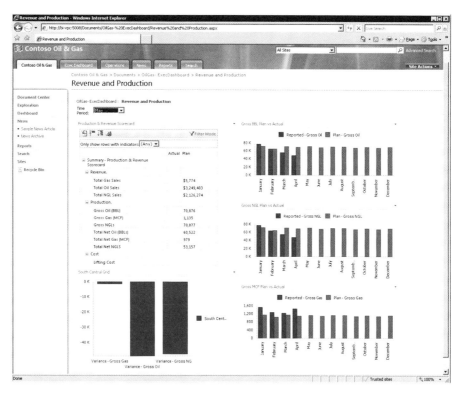

EXHIBIT 15.59 Category: Tactical Dashboard; Industry: Energy (oil and gas); Functional/Organizational Level: Executive

Source: Reprinted with permission from Microsoft Corporation.

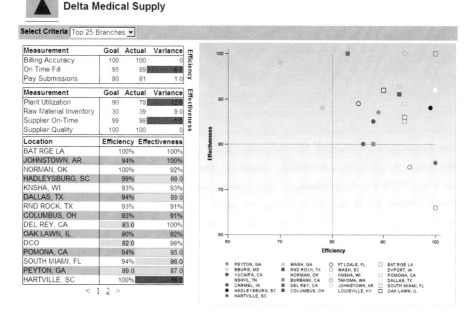

EXHIBIT 15.60 Category: Tactical Dashboard; Industry: Manufacturing; Functional/Organizational Level: Production

Source: This Visual Mining NetCharts Software product screenshot reprinted with permission of Visual Mining, Inc. © 2007 Visual Mining. All Rights Reserved.

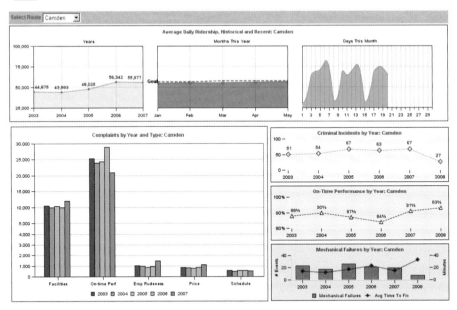

EXHIBIT 15.61 Category: Operational Dashboard; Industry: Transportation; Functional/Organizational Level: Executive

Source: This Visual Mining NetCharts Software product screenshot reprinted with permission of Visual Mining, Inc. © 2007 Visual Mining. All Rights Reserved.

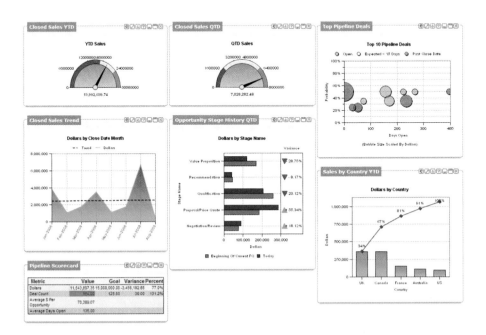

EXHIBIT 15.62 Category: Operational Dashboard; Industry: Nonspecific; Functional/Organizational Level: Sales (CRM)

Source: This Visual Mining NetCharts Software product screenshot reprinted with permission of Visual Mining, Inc. © 2007 Visual Mining. All Rights Reserved.

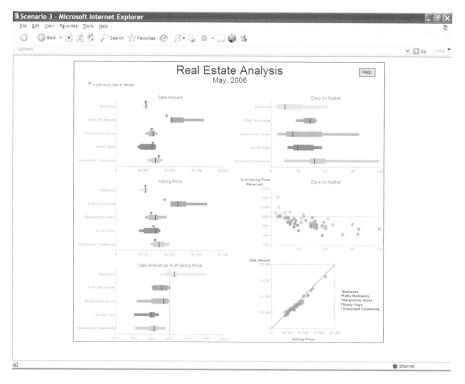

EXHIBIT 15.63 Category: Operational Dashboard; Industry: Real Estate; Functional/Organizational Level: Sales

Source: Used with permission of Visual-io.

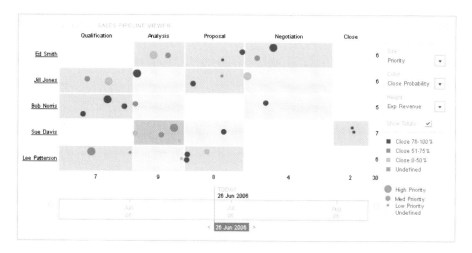

EXHIBIT 15.64 Category: Operational Dashboard; Industry: Nonspecific; Functional/Organizational Level: Sales (CRM)

Source: Used with permission of Robert Allison.

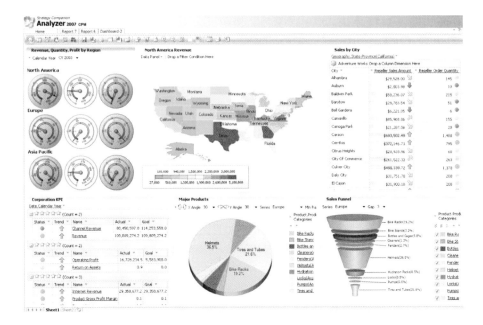

EXHIBIT 15.65 Category: Operational Dashboard; Industry: Nonspecific; Functional/Organizational Level: Sales

Source: Used with permission of Strategy Companion.

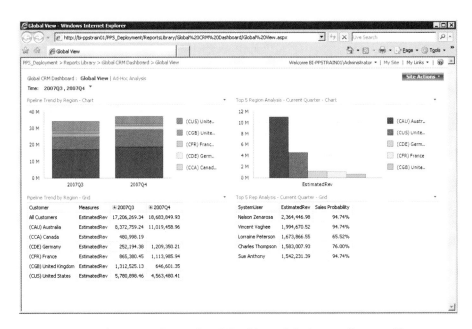

EXHIBIT 15.66 Category: Operational Dashboard; Industry: Nonspecific; Functional/Organizational Level: Sales (CRM)

Source: Printed with permission—Solver, Inc. (www.solverusa.com)

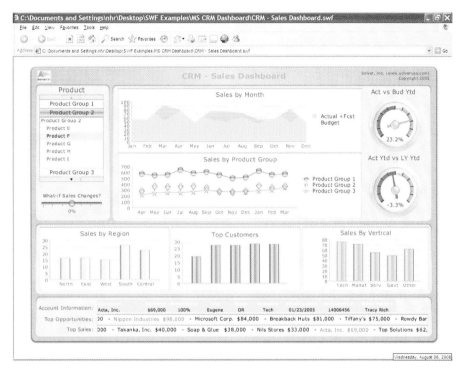

EXHIBIT 15.67 Category: Operational Dashboard; Industry: Nonspecific; Functional/Organizational Level: Sales (CRM)

Source: Printed with permission—Solver, Inc. (www.solverusa.com).

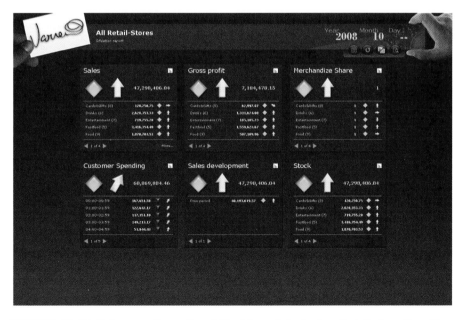

EXHIBIT 15.68 Category: Operational Dashboard; Industry: Retail; Functional/Organizational Level: Sales

Source: Reprinted with permission from ProfitBase.

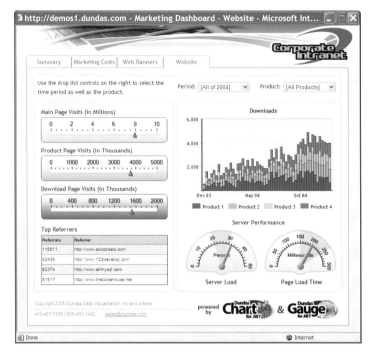

EXHIBIT 15.69 Category: Operational Dashboard; Industry: Nonspecific; Functional/Organizational Level: Marketing (online)
Source: Dashboard provided courtesy of Dundas Data Visualization—www.dundas.com.

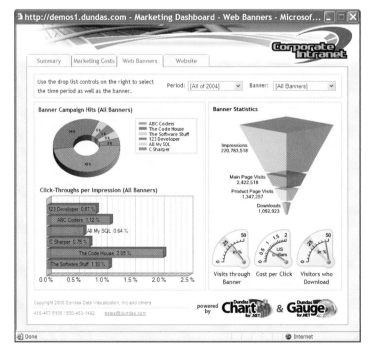

EXHIBIT 15.70 Category: Operational Dashboard; Industry: Nonspecific; Functional/Organizational Level: Marketing (online)
Source: Dashboard provided courtesy of Dundas Data Visualization—www.dundas.com.

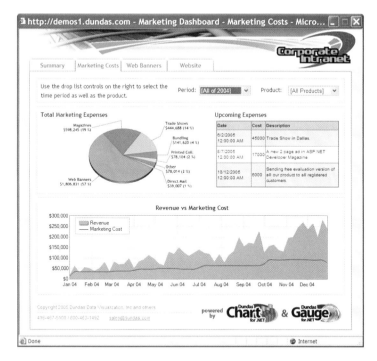

EXHIBIT 15.71 Category: Operational Dashboard; Industry: Nonspecific; Functional/Organizational Level: Marketing (online)

Source: Dashboard provided courtesy of Dundas Data Visualization— www.dundas.com.

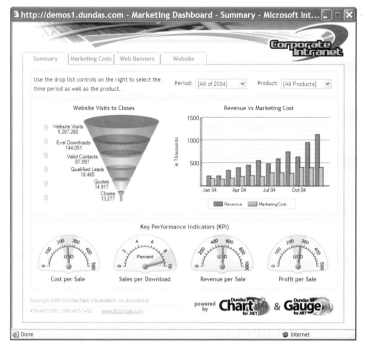

EXHIBIT 15.72 Category: Operational Dashboard; Industry: Nonspecific; Functional/Organizational Level: Marketing (online)

Source: Dashboard provided courtesy of Dundas Data Visualization— www.dundas.com.

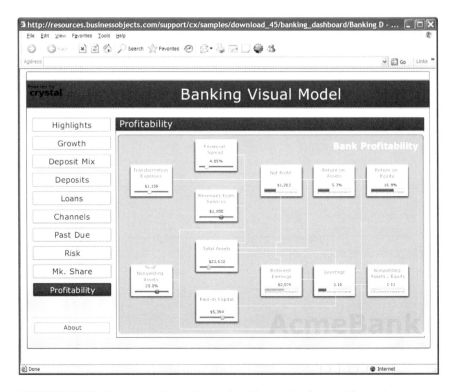

EXHIBIT 15.73 Category: Operational Dashboard; Industry: Financial Services (bank); Functional/Organizational Level: Finance

Source: Used with permission of Business Objects Americas.

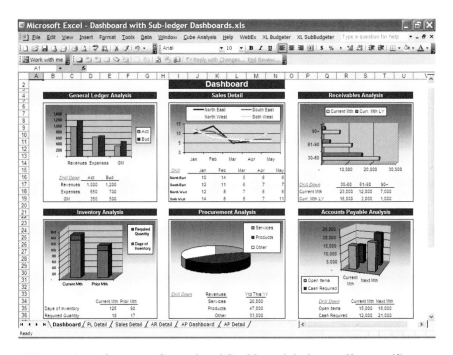

EXHIBIT 15.74 Category: Operational Dashboard; Industry: Nonspecific; Functional/Organizational Level: Finance

Source: Printed with permission—Solver, Inc. (www.solverusa.com).

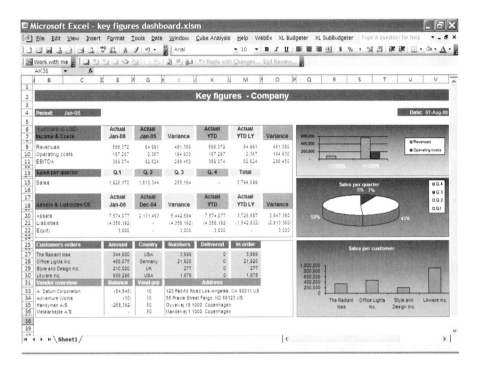

EXHIBIT 15.75 Category: Operational Dashboard; Industry: Nonspecific; Functional/Organizational Level: Finance
Source: Printed with permission—Solver, Inc. (www.solverusa.com).

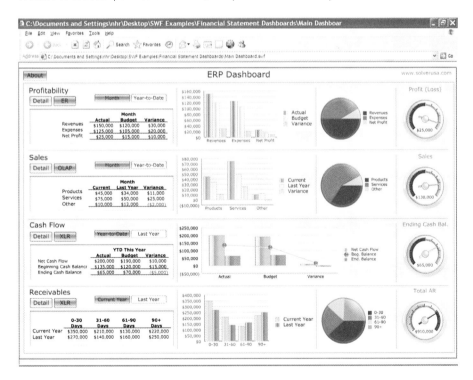

EXHIBIT 15.76 Category: Operational Dashboard; Industry: Nonspecific; Functional/Organizational Level: Finance
Source: Printed with permission—Solver, Inc. (www.solverusa.com).

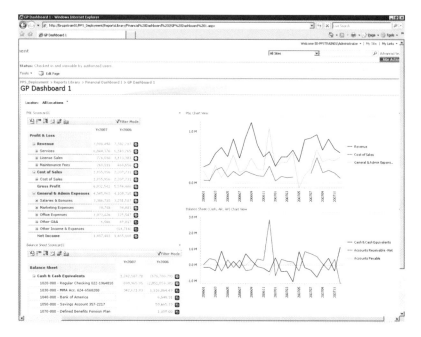

EXHIBIT 15.77 Category: Operational Dashboard; Industry: Nonspecific; Functional/Organizational Level: Finance

Source: Printed with permission—Solver, Inc. (www.solverusa.com).

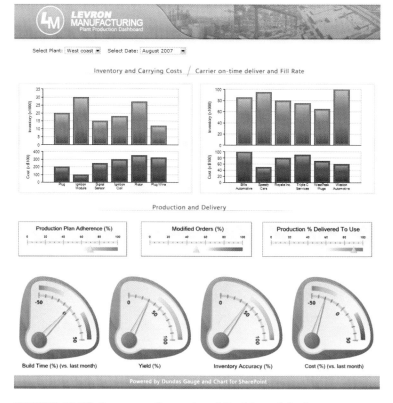

EXHIBIT 15.78 Category: Operational Dashboard; Industry: Manufacturing; Functional/Organizational Level: Operations

Source: Dashboard provided courtesy of Dundas Data Visualization—www.undas.com.

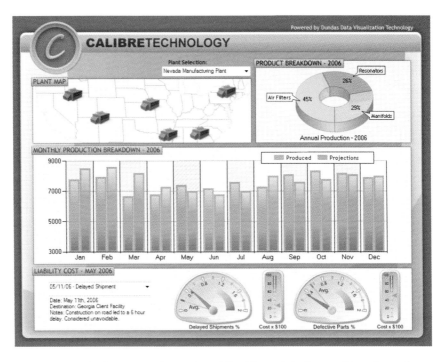

EXHIBIT 15.79 Category: Operational Dashboard; Industry: Manufacturing; Functional/Organizational Level: Operations

Source: Dashboard provided courtesy of Dundas Data Visualization—www.dundas.com.

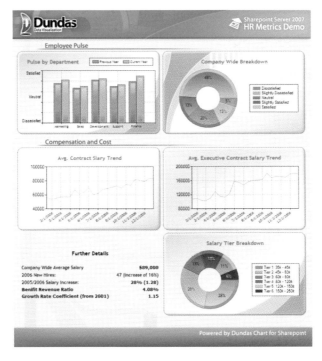

EXHIBIT 15.80 Category: Operational Dashboard; Industry: Nonspecific; Functional/Organizational Level: Human Resources

Source: Dashboard provided courtesy of Dundas Data Visualization—www.dundas.com.

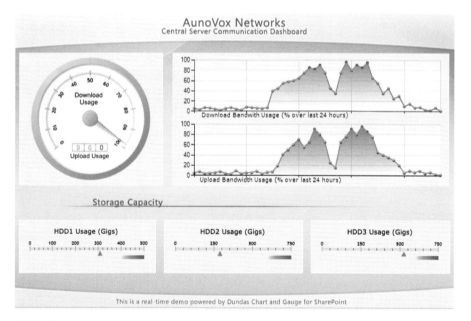

EXHIBIT 15.81 Category: Operational Dashboard; Industry: Nonspecific; Functional/Organizational Level: Information Technology

Source: Dashboard provided courtesy of Dundas Data Visualization—www.dundas.com.

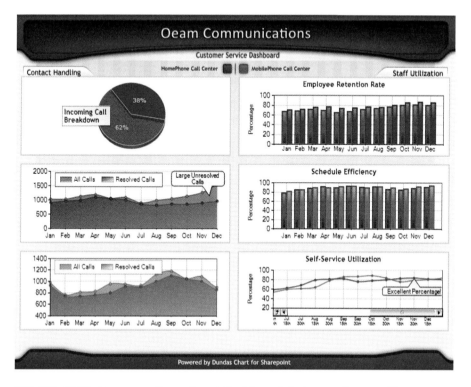

EXHIBIT 15.82 Category: Operational Dashboard; Industry: Nonspecific; Functional/Organizational Level: Customer Service

Source: Dashboard provided courtesy of Dundas Data Visualization—www.dundas.com.

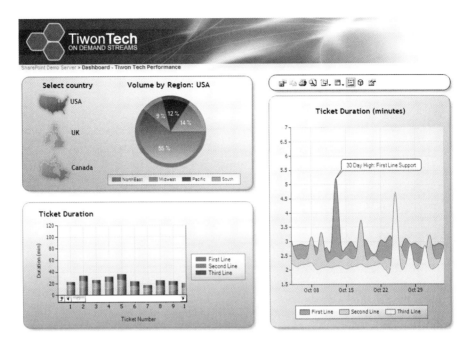

EXHIBIT 15.83 Category: Operational Dashboard; Industry: Nonspecific; Functional/Organizational Level: Customer Service

Source: Dashboard provided courtesy of Dundas Data Visualization—www.dundas.com.

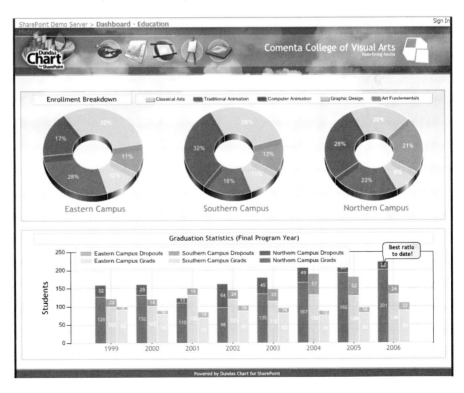

EXHIBIT 15.84 Category: Operational Dashboard; Industry: Education; Functional/Organizational Level: Student Relations

Source: Copyright © 2008 LiveData, Inc. All rights reserved—www.livedata.com.

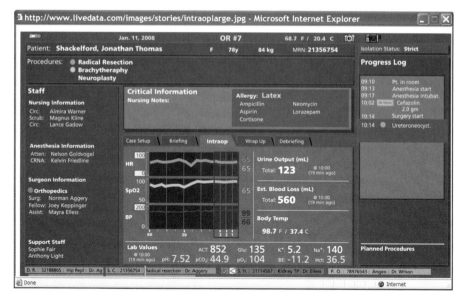

EXHIBIT 15.85 Category: Operational Dashboard; Industry: Healthcare; Functional/Organizational Level: Hospital (patient care)

Source: Dashboard provided courtesy of Dundas Data Visualization—www.dundas.com.

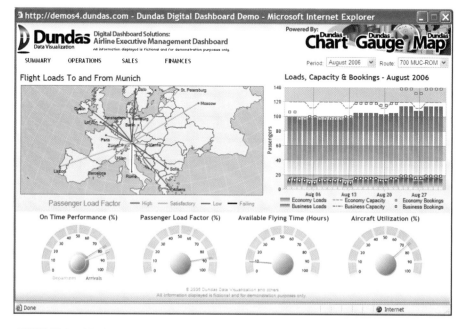

EXHIBIT 15.86 Category: Operational Dashboard; Industry: Transportation Functional/Organizational Level: Operations

Source: Dashboard provided courtesy of Dundas Data Visualization—www.dundas.com.

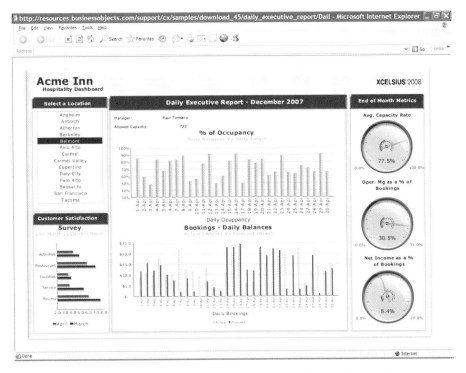

EXHIBIT 15.87 Category: Operational Dashboard; Industry: Hospitality; Functional/Organizational Level: Operations

Source: Used with permission of Business Objects Americas.

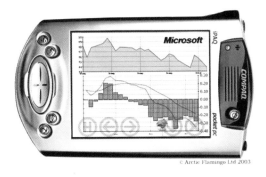

EXHIBIT 15.88 Category: Operational Dashboard; Industry: Nonspecific; Functional/Organizational Level: Mobile

Source: Reprinted with permission from Microsoft Corporation.

EXHIBIT 15.89 Category: Operational Dashboard; Industry: Nonspecific; Functional/Organizational Level: Mobile

Source: Copyright Webalo, Inc.—The Webalo Mobile Dashboard for anywhere, any time, on-demand delivery of enterprise data to mobile devices.

EXHIBIT 15.90 Category: Operational Dashboard; Industry: Nonspecific; Functional/Organizational Level: Operations

Source: Reprinted with permission from ProfitBase.

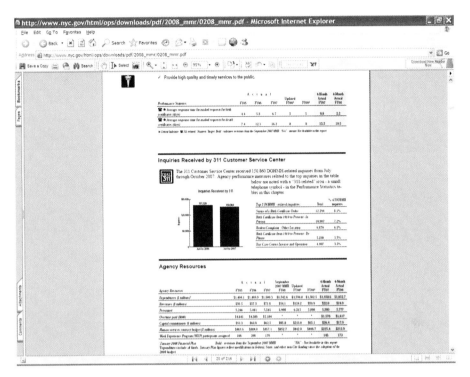

EXHIBIT 15.91 Category: Operational Dashboard; Industry: Public Sector; Functional/Organizational Level: Customer Service

Source: Used with the permission of the City of New York. ©2008 New York City Department of Information Technology and Telecommunications. All Rights Reserved.

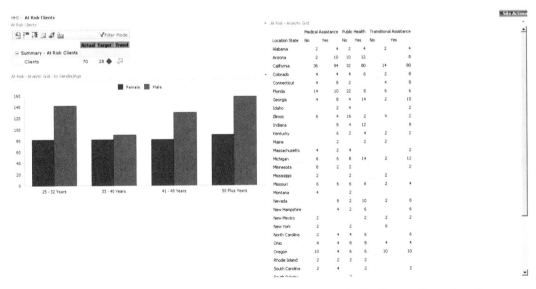

EXHIBIT 15.92 Category: Operational Dashboard; Industry: Public Sector; Functional/Organizational Level: Healthcare

Source: Reprinted with permission from Microsoft Corporation.

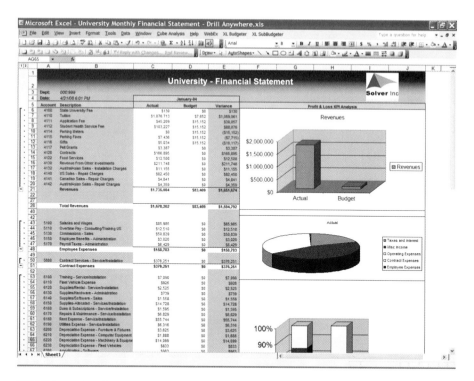

EXHIBIT 15.93 Category: Operational Dashboard; Industry: Education; Functional/Organizational Level: Finance

Source: Printed with permission—Solver, Inc. (www.solverusa.com).

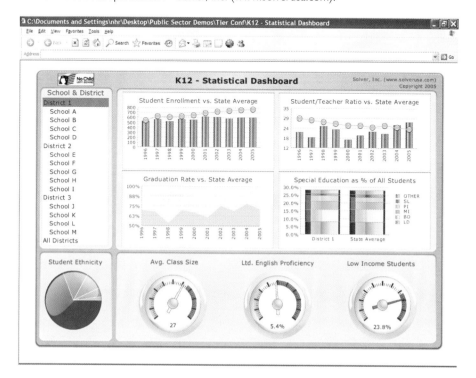

EXHIBIT 15.94 Category: Operational Dashboard; Industry: Education (K-12); Functional/Organizational Level: Academic

Source: Printed with permission—Solver, Inc. (www.solverusa.com).

EXHIBIT 15.95 Category: Operational Dashboard; Industry: Financial (bank); Functional/Organizational Level: Executive

Source: Used with permission of Business Objects Americas.

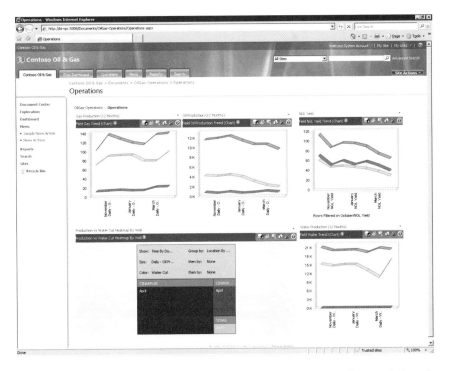

EXHIBIT 15.96 Category: Operational Dashboard; Industry: Energy (oil and gas); Functional/Organizational Level: Operations

Source: Reprinted with permission from Microsoft Corporation.

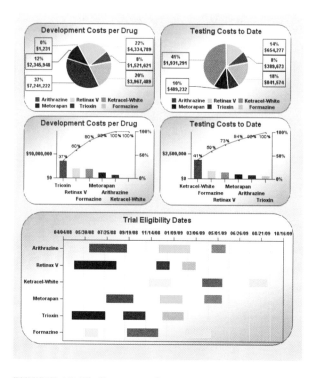

EXHIBIT 15.97 Category: Operational Dashboard; Industry: Pharmaceutical; Functional/Organizational Level: Financial

Source: This Visual Mining NetCharts Software product screenshot reprinted with permission of Visual Mining, Inc. © 2007 Visual Mining. All Rights Reserved.

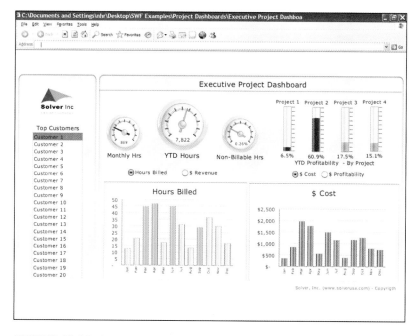

EXHIBIT 15.98 Category: Operational Dashboard; Industry: Nonspecific; Functional/Organizational Level: Project Management

Source: Printed with permission—Solver, Inc. (www.solverusa.com).

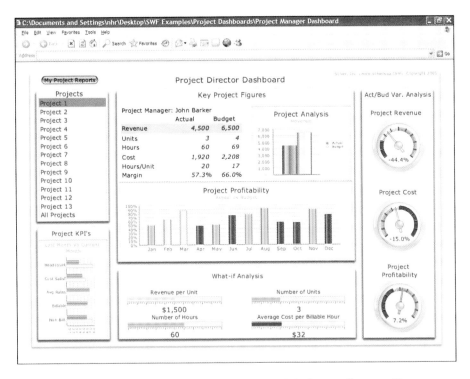

EXHIBIT 15.99 Category: Operational Dashboard; Industry: Nonspecific; Functional/Organizational Level: Project Management

Source: Printed with permission—Solver, Inc. (www.solverusa.com).

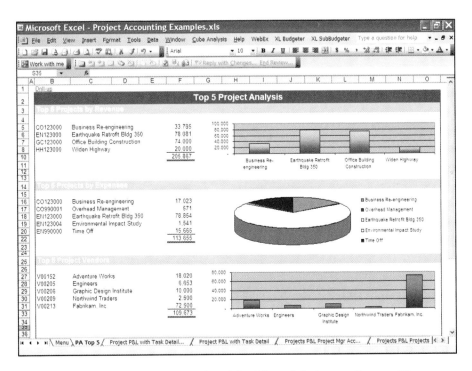

EXHIBIT 15.100 Category: Operational Dashboard; Industry: Nonspecific; Functional/Organizational Level: Project Management

Source: Printed with permission—Solver, Inc. (www.solverusa.com).

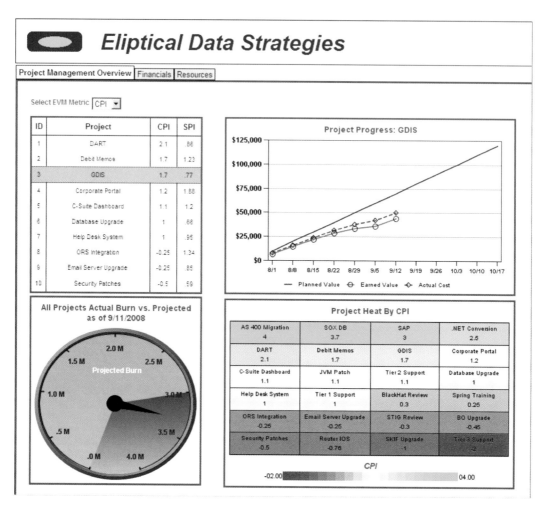

EXHIBIT 15.101 Category: Operational Dashboard; Industry: Nonspecific; Functional/Organizational Level: Project Management

Source: This Visual Mining NetCharts Software product screenshot reprinted with permission of Visual Mining, Inc. © 2007 Visual Mining. All Rights Reserved.

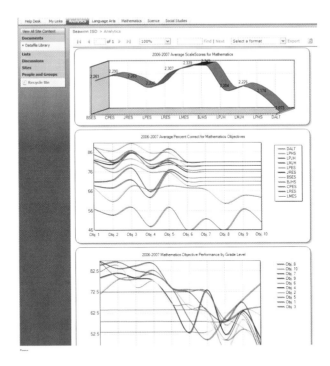

EXHIBIT 15.102 Category: Operational Dashboard; Industry: Education (K-12); Functional/Organizational Level: Administration (curriculum)

Source: Reprinted with permission from Seawinn, Inc. 2009.

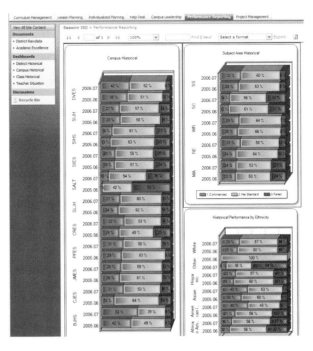

EXHIBIT 15.103 Category: Operational Dashboard; Industry: Education (K-12); Functional/Organizational Level: Administration (school level)

Source: Reprinted with permission from Seawinn, Inc. 2009.

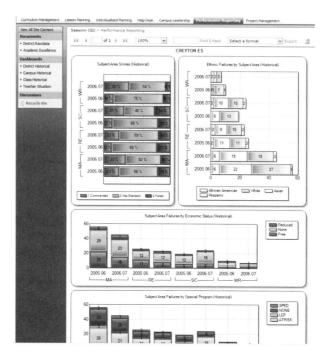

EXHIBIT 15.104 Category: Operational Dashboard; Industry: Education (K-12); Functional/Organizational Level: Principal (campus level)

Source: Reprinted with permission from Seawinn, Inc. 2009.

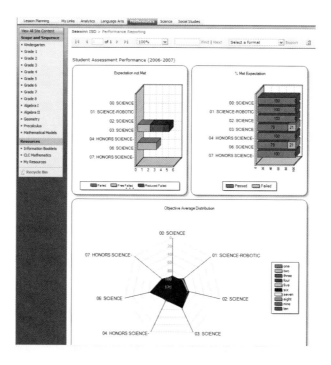

EXHIBIT 15.105 Category: Operational Dashboard; Industry: Education (K-12); Functional/Organizational Level: Teacher (class level)

Source: Reprinted with permission from Seawinn, Inc. 2009.

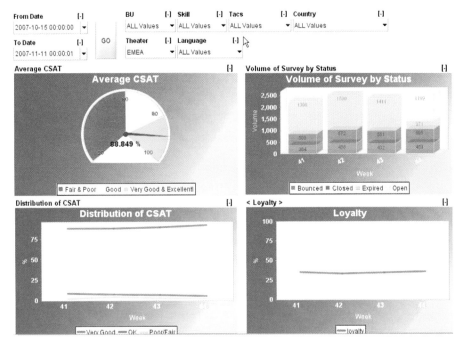

EXHIBIT 15.106 Category: Operational Dashboard; Industry: Nonspecific; Functional/Organizational Level: Operations

Source: Reprinted with permission from InfoCaptor.

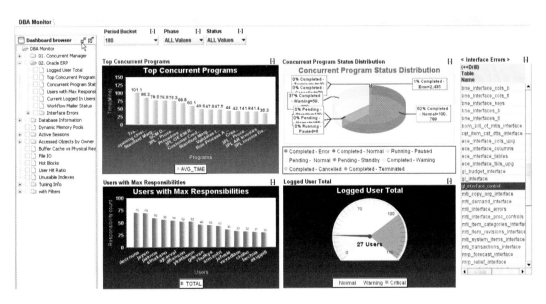

EXHIBIT 15.107 Category: Operational Dashboard; Industry: Nonspecific; Functional/Organizational Level: Information Technology

Source: Reprinted with permission from InfoCaptor.

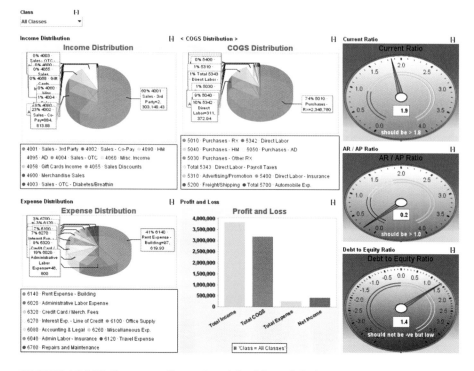

EXHIBIT 15.108 Category: Operational Dashboard; Industry: Nonspecific; Functional/Organizational Level: Finance
Source: Reprinted with permission from InfoCaptor.

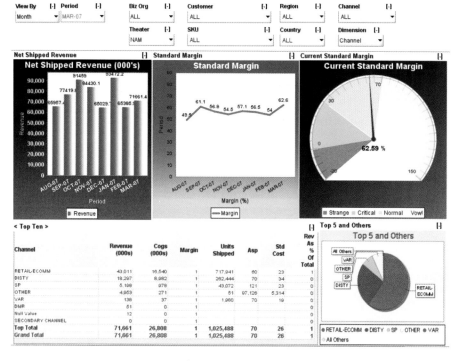

EXHIBIT 15.109 Category: Operational Dashboard; Industry: Retail; Functional/ Organizational Level: Sales
Source: Reprinted with permission from InfoCaptor.

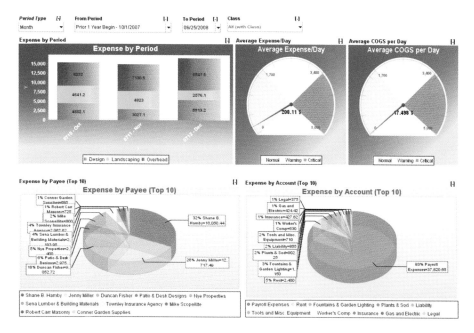

EXHIBIT 15.110 Category: Operational Dashboard; Industry: Nonspecific; Functional/Organizational Level: Finance

Source: Reprinted with permission from InfoCaptor.

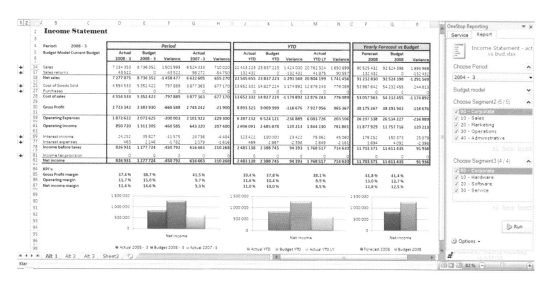

EXHIBIT 15.111 Category: Operational Dashboard; Industry: Nonspecific; Functional/ Organizational Level: Finance

Source: Reprinted with permission from OneStop Reporting.

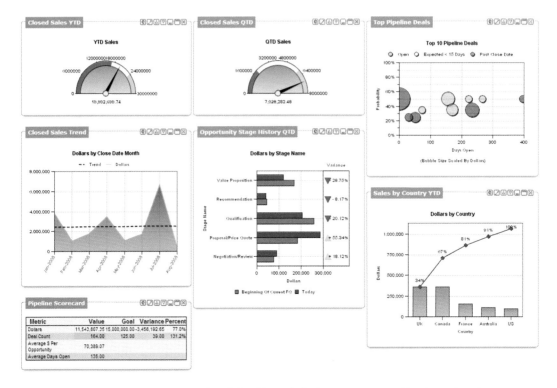

EXHIBIT 15.112 Category: Operational Dashboard; Industry: Nonspecific; Functional/ Organizational Level: Sales (CRM)

Source: This Visual Mining NetCharts Software product screenshot reprinted with permission of Visual Mining, Inc. © 2007 Visual Mining. All Rights Reserved.

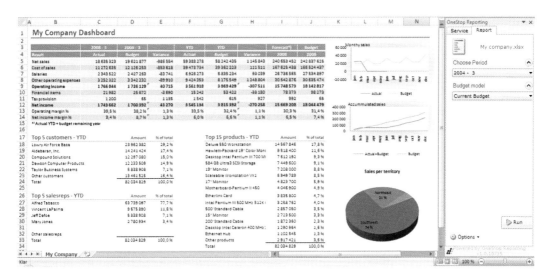

EXHIBIT 15.113 Category: Operational Dashboard; Industry: Nonspecific; Functional/ Organizational Level: Finance

Source: Reprinted with permission from OneStop Reporting.

PART 3   SUMMARY AND READINESS CHECKLIST

This part has discussed the importance of a structured design process and has provided an example showing how to organize your own dashboard design activities. Some key design tips were then offered for achieving the best possible layout for your dashboards. Finally, it was described how to conduct a storyboard session to optimize the dashboard layout process. Chapter 15 provided a large library of dashboard examples to give you ideas and insights into the look and feel of various dashboards and the related technologies.

Whereas Part 1 introduced you to dashboards and metrics and Part 2 discussed various architecture options that can drive a dashboard solution, the goal of Part 3 has been to give you the tools you need to decide on the types of dashboards you should be providing to your organization. You should now be ready to proceed to Part 4, which will help you organize your project to ensure a successful implementation.

The checklist that follows summarizes some of the key topics you have read about in the chapters in this part and lets you score your skills:

Scoring: Not Sure = 1 point, Basic understanding = 2 points, Clear understanding = 3 points

	Score
☐ Understand the three dashboard categories	
☐ What is a storyboard?	
☐ Manage the storyboard process	
☐ Use the most readable fonts	
☐ Use of colors	
☐ Prioritize and select metrics	
☐ Select the dashboard components that work best	
☐ Use dashboard real estate effectively	
☐ Gather ideas from dashboard examples	
☐ Use parameters to limit data sets	
Total Score	

Place your total score in the right box in the following Scorecard:

Status	Points	Color	Your Score
Ready	21–30	⬤	
In Progress	15–20	⬤	
Not Ready	0–15	⬤	

PART 4

MANAGING A DASHBOARD PROJECT

The first three parts of this book covered everything from the definitions of dashboard, metrics, and key performance indicators to architecture design and associated considerations. In addition, several dashboard examples were given from various industries in Part 3. Now is the time to learn more about managing the implementation of a dashboard project. This part will provide you with some insight into the lessons learnt from real-world implementations and should serve as a practical reference if you are planning to start a dashboard implementation project.

Planning the Project

16

W hat does a dashboard project look like? What resources are needed to implement a dashboard project? Are these projects simple or too complex? The answer to these questions lies in another question: How much information do you need in these dashboards? If you are looking for basic dashboards with static information, that would be regarded as a simple project. If you are looking for interactive dashboards that will provide some details (second-level information), that would be regarded as a project of medium complexity. However, if you are looking for highly interactive dashboards that will allow you to perform deep analysis via drillthrough and cross-drill capabilities, that would be regarded as a project of high complexity.

Whether you are about to embark on a simple, mid-level, or complex dashboard project, it is essential to plan your project well. For discussion purposes, we will assume that it is your responsibility to lead or evangelize the dashboard project in your company. Whether you are leading this project as director of information technology (IT), as vice president of operations, as manager of finance, or simply as a project manager, the first and most important step is to know the audience (users) of these dashboards. Once you know the users, the second most important step is to know the requirements of those users.

In our experience most of the companies start with a dashboard project for one department or a few users—for example, the chief executive officer (CEO), chief financial officer (CFO), or department heads—and later expand it to other areas. This approach works well from a development and user-adoption perspective; in our experience, however, many companies fail to take the holistic view of long-term needs when they undertake the project. They may start the project for one department not knowing the requirements of other departments. Or they may start the project for the CEO or the CFO as the user, considering their requirements only as being given the information that they currently receive in the form of reports. In the current business world, the interdependencies between various departments or functions of a company are increasing by the day. C-level executives and department or function heads are always looking for better quality of information that allows for analysis as opposed to canned reports. In order to get the most out of your dashboard project, it is imperative that you understand these interdependencies and information needs, at least at the functional (metrics) level if not at the data level.

Based on our experience, we would say that the planning phase is where it all begins. Make sure to allocate enough time in your project schedule to ensure that this critical step is not rushed. First the project team members must be identified and their roles clearly defined. Who will be the executive sponsor? What are the overall project objectives? It is not uncommon for the primary users (i.e., executives or line-of-business managers) to play a limited role in the dashboard development. Therefore, the team members must have access to and gain insight into the needs and wants of this group.

In the planning phase, team members determine the scope of the project. What key performance indicators (KPIs) are important to the primary users? What data is needed to support the KPIs, and where is that data located? A dashboard is most useful if the metrics will be measured against predefined conditions and thresholds. What are these conditions and thresholds?

If you are working within a tight timeline, populating the dashboard is of utmost concern. Take care not to underestimate the complexity of the databases in which the data resides. The tremendous flexibility enterprise applications provide for customization results in data tables that are very complex. Accessing the data from a myriad of tables is not a simple task; it requires technical resources with detailed knowledge of the underlying table structure and database skill. It can take days to gather the data relevant for a single KPI, so plan accordingly.

Budget plays a major role in defining the scope of the project. The work required to create custom queries to provide the desired metrics might be out of budget. Set realistic goals for your dashboard project by striking a balance between the primary users' needs and what you can afford to deliver. Determine up front which KPIs are critical and stick to the plan.

It is recommended that the project start with a discovery phase, also called an envisioning phase. This phase helps you lay the foundation and establish the right direction for your dashboard project. You should then gather requirements from each user or user group as applicable. After finishing the requirements phase, make sure you get a sign-off on requirements before you proceed into the design phase. Validate the design with the customers' chief architect to ensure there will be no surprises later. Once validated, you should then kick off the build phase. After the application has been built, typically you should get an acceptance from the users (User Acceptance Testing) before deploying it to the masses. In the following sections, these project phases are discussed briefly as they relate to a dashboard project.

PROJECT PHASES

Discovery or Requirements Gathering and Proof of Concept

Once the scope of the dashboard project has been defined and the plan is in place, the process of requirements gathering begins. Interview the key stakeholders to determine their needs and expectations for the dashboard. These needs and expectations should map to the KPIs.

Discuss the options available for dashboard presentation and functionality. A dashboard provides the user with a number of different ways to graphically display the data. This is the time to cover personal preferences (e.g., top-level navigation, use of bar charts, gauges, etc.). For each dashboard, the desired data elements must be identified. Relationships between them must be defined so that appropriate drill-down and drill-around capabilities can be provided. These drill-down and drill-around capabilities are important to know upfront, so that the design, especially of the online analytical processing (OLAP) cubes, can be successfully implemented.

Some tools and technologies lend themselves well to prototyping and iterative development. Taking advantage of those capabilities can increase the likelihood that the final dashboard meets the users' expectations.

Design

Once the requirements for the content and appearance of the dashboard have been agreed on, major aspects of the design must be completed:

- Refine the user interface and control flow.
- Confirm the data sources for each data element.
- Determine how to "persist" data when historical trending information is desired, but not available from the transaction database.
- Define the queries needed to retrieve each data element.
- Determine drill paths.
- Design the overall architecture and structure of OLAP cubes.

Further details on solution architecture can be found in Part Two.

Build and Validate

The "real" development begins at this stage of the project. Several tasks occur here, typically in parallel, closely coordinated with each other:

- *Front-end storyboarding*. Create the dashboard user interface. Final user interface decisions must be made. Personal preferences have been discussed, but now is the time to evaluate the graph and chart types that best represent the data to be displayed. In addition, make decisions regarding grouping data to provide the greatest visibility for cross analysis. What visual alerts, such as color changes when values exceed expected thresholds, will be defined? Have a game plan in place for when these thresholds are surpassed. Which "summary-detail" options will be provided? How much interactive drilling to other graphs or charts will be available?

- *Query implementation*. Create the queries to retrieve the necessary information from the appropriate databases. This step can be particularly complex and time consuming, especially if there are multiple data sources for the various data elements in the dashboard. This is especially true if those data sources include customized enterprise resource planning (ERP), customer relationship management (CRM), or supply chain management enterprise applications that generally have complex database schemas. Writing advanced SQL statements is a challenging task for even the skilled programmer.

- *Data warehouse and cube development*. Once the queries are written to bring data from databases or source systems, build the data warehouse where all the data comes together. Then develop the OLAP cubes based on the design to best address drill-down capabilities needed by the users.

- *Dashboard development and publishing*. Design the dashboard layout and pick the right charts and reports. Connect the dashboard to the OLAP cubes or other sources depending on where the data is coming for the chart or report. Publish the dashboard to a portal where users will access it.

- *Configure security*. Security rules must be implemented for the dashboard to display the appropriate information for various users. To minimize the need for redundant administration, those security rules should take advantage of security frameworks that are already being managed.

- *Dashboard validation*. As with any software project, when the effort reaches "code complete," it must be tested to ensure that it meets the requirements and specifications outlined in the project plan. Some of this validation can be done independently by the technical team. Other aspects, especially ensuring that the data is correct, must be done by the primary users of the dashboard or their representatives.

Deploy

Once the dashboard has been built and tested, it is deployed into production. Security requirements must be implemented in the production environment. Integration within a corporate network environment must be completed (including considerations for portal frameworks, extranets for partner and customer access, etc.).

Maintain

With the dashboard in production or "live," steps must be taken to provide for ongoing maintenance. Over time, requirements and expectations for the dashboard will change. The dashboard solution should be flexible and open to allow for such inevitable enhancement requests. If the dashboard was implemented by a vendor or solution provider, knowledge transfer to the customer for ongoing maintenance is essential. To minimize reliance on external resources, tools to promote self-sufficiency are beneficial.

PROJECT PLANNING: KEY STEPS

In general, the following steps serve as a useful guideline for planning a dashboard project:

1. Ensure that the project is backed by senior management.
2. Define how dashboard project will help your organization in meeting current challenges.
3. Define project goals.
4. Define high-level project scope.
5. Define the project team's structure and roles.
6. Identify team members for each role.
7. Develop high-level project plan.
8. Gather requirements:
   a. Immediate requirements
   b. Short-term requirements
   c. Long-term requirements
9. Define the conceptual dashboard design (primarily, information and linkages).
10. Define the high-level technical architecture that supports the conceptual design.
11. Present a conceptual design to target users for feedback and validation:
   a. Hold a joint session with various users in one room.

    b. Facilitate the session so as to trigger the participants' thinking to better articulate their information needs for analysis.

12. Adjust the conceptual design based on the outcome of the sessions listed here.

13. Validate and/or adjust the technical architecture based on the new conceptual design.

14. Initiate the implementation following the famous scrum methodology[1]:

    a. Define multiple sprints (one functional area could be one sprint).

    b. Develop an application for each sprint (each sprint could have one or more dashboards); each sprint will typically include phases such as design, develop, and test.

    c. Within each sprint, provide regular updates (presentations) to the users.

    d. Upon completion of each sprint (or dashboard), get the sign-off from the users.

15. Test the overall application.

16. Facilitate a user acceptance test.

17. Deploy the application.

18. Train the users and power users.

19. Stabilize the application.

20. Monitor usage of dashboards by users (user adoption).

21. After a few months, conduct survey of users to determine whether the current dashboards meet their requirements.

22. Enhance the application (if needed) based on users' increased need for information and/or analysis.

The size of the implementation team will vary depending on the complexity of the dashboard project. Exhibit 16.1 is a sample of the roles that we believe are typically required to implement a dashboard project.

Exhibit 16.2 contains a sample project plan for your reference. This is a generic plan that can serve as a guideline while you plan for your dashboard project. As you will notice, it is a good practice to allocate time for requirements analysis and design in the initial stages of the project. This is especially important in the dashboard projects because the foundation of a dashboard design is laid in the design phase. It is essential for the solution architect to understand various aspects of your business, their relationships to each other, and the important metrics that you will be tracking, given that this information will be used directly by the solution architect to design the data warehouse structure. For more details, see Part Two.

Note

1. Scrum is an iterative incremental process of software development or software project implementation.

Resource Role	Role Description	% Time (of project duration)
Project Manager	• Responsible for meeting project goals and timelines • Communication with steering committee • Project status reporting • Responsible to drive the issues to resolution by mobilizing the Subject Matter Expert's • Provide leadership and direction to the team	20%
Business Analyst	• Lead and facilitate requirements gathering • Lead and facilitate the process of identifying the KPIs that must be monitored • Spearhead the design process working closely with the application and data warehouse team members	50%-60%
Application Specialist	• Installation of dashboard application and readiness of various environments (development, production, and test) • Application design • Application configuration • Facilitate JAD (joint application design) sessions	70%-80%
Data Warehouse Specialist	• Responsible to map source systems to the dashboard application • Integration design • Data warehouse and OLAP cube design • Assist the application specialist in design and delivery	70%-80%

EXHIBIT 16.1 Sample Project Team Roles for a Dashboard Project

EXHIBIT 16.2 Sample Project Plan for a Dashboard Project Implementation

Engaging the Users

17

W hile dashboards look very fancy and attractive, their real usage and adoption can be tricky. Executives and managers become so used to the old-fashioned reports that they typically show a resistance to change. Are you surprised or wondering why, knowing that dashboards could provide so much richer information in one place? Executives, in most cases, receive information in the form of printed reports at their desks without spending a single minute on producing them. After the deployment of dashboards, they are usually required to access this information with a few clicks, which requires them to spend at least some time to extract the information they are looking for. This often requires some training and getting used to. Undoubtedly, they will receive better quality information at their fingertips with these dashboard tools, but usage will be heavily dependent on the user's interest. Interest in the dashboard application generally governs whether the users will support the dashboard project initiative. Hence, it is critical to create users' interest in dashboards and gain their support before even starting the project, and this calls for a well-structured project kick-off. This will keep users engaged throughout the project implementation as well as after deployment. It will also help facilitate faster user adoption, which is another challenge that organizations often find difficult to overcome once the dashboard application has been implemented.

BUILDING USER SUPPORT AND INTEREST

If users are not excited about and interested in using dashboards, their usage will be limited and the dashboards either die over a period of time or become a static report with little or no enhancement. Therefore, as a dashboard project lead it is essential that you invest enough time and energy to build users' support and interest in dashboards—you must help users understand how dashboards will benefit them in making better decisions faster and at the right time. So, how should you plan to get users excited about a new dashboard tool? Here are a few steps that should help you gain the support of users and arouse their interest in such a project and even motivate them to serve as evangelists for dashboards:

Step 1. Communication is the key:

- Define what dashboards can and cannot do.
- Explain why your company plans to deploy such a tool.
- Explain how this will affect their day-to-day lives.
- Explain the deployment plan.
- Explain what will be expected from them and what they can contribute.

Step 2. Identify key users who will be benefited by availability of richer information.

Step 3. Assign a role to them (e.g., dashboard guru for department ABC, etc.).

Step 4. Assign some tasks to them, requesting contributions to the project in the form of user requirements.

Step 5. Request them to explain the importance of dashboards within their functions or departments to other, secondary users.

Step 6. Invite them to the project kick-off meeting.

Step 7. Walk through the project milestones.

Step 8. Invite them to joint application design (JAD) sessions.

Step 9. Provide them with periodic updates as project progresses.

Step 10. Invite them to walkthrough sessions where samples of dashboards are presented. This will also allow them to provide feedback.

Step 11. Invite them to user acceptance testing sessions.

Step 12. Walk through the training and deployment plan.

PROJECT KICK-OFF

As we all know, "a good start is winning half the battle," and for any project a good kick-off is like ensuring half of its success. We always recommend kicking off the project with a nicely structured PowerPoint presentation, taking the audience through the stepped approach that will be followed to execute this project. Provide users with a high-level picture of the project goals, key milestones, what is expected of them, and so forth.

Present a project implementation methodology that you will follow. Exhibit 17.1 provides illustration of a typical implementation methodology.

As the project lead, you must explain the standard implementation approach as discussed previously and then walk them through the tailored approach that you plan to take for this particular dashboard project (see Exhibit 17.2).

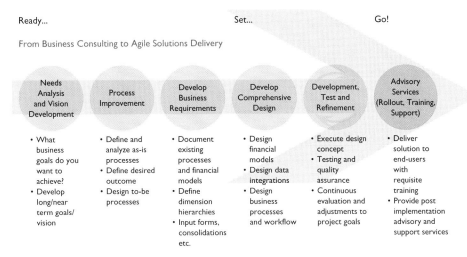

EXHIBIT 17.1 Sample Implementation Methodology for Dashboard Project

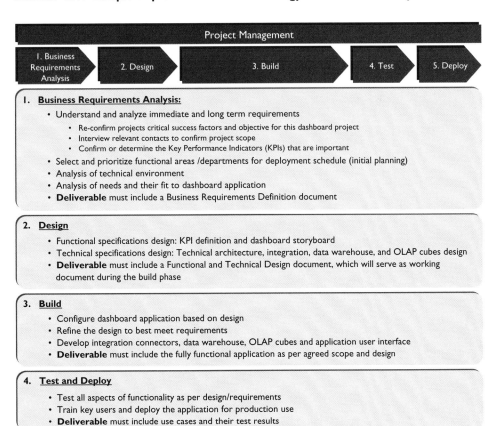

EXHIBIT 17.2 Sample Implementation Approach for a Dashboard Project

- **Pain Points or Problem Areas**
  - o Ability to access the data
  - o Time taken to report on this data
  - o Ability to analyze
  - o Ability to drill down to details
  - o Ability to have cross-functional views of same data (single version of the truth)

- **Functional Focus**
  - o Finance
  - o Marketing
  - o Sales
  - o Call center (service)

- **BI Requirements Wish List**
  - o Sales
    - Sales pipeline report (twenty different pages required for different views)
    - Sales by customer view
    - Sales by product view
    - Backlog orders/inventory view
  - o Finance
    - Plan vs. actual budget report
    - Profit and loss report
  - o Call Center
    - Number of calls per month by problem type
    - Number of calls per month by product category
    - Time per call by problem type

EXHIBIT 17.3 Sample of Initial Requirements Gathering

Before the project kick-off takes place, most of you must have gathered some basic information about your customers' (users') needs and current issues. Document these issues (pain points) and requirements and present them to the users to confirm your understanding of their needs and pain points. Depending on the nature of this meeting, you could leverage this session to confirm, add, or modify these points (see Exhibit 17.3).

Once you have explained the high-level items (e.g., project goals, milestones, and your understanding of requirements), you may want to consider showing some relevant examples of the dashboards. If the users are from the sales department, therefore, you may want to present some dashboard examples related to sales. This is an effective way to get users quickly and deeply involved in the project, as it helps your audience visualize the end result of the project you are about to start.

chapter 18

Project Tips

We all know that it is the project manager's primary responsibility to manage the scope, duration, and cost triangle, set up a baseline project plan, track to milestones and report status. But to manage projects successfully in a consulting context requires additional seasoning, whether you are an external consultant or an internal champion serving as the project manager.

In the following section we have listed some of the top ten "Do's" based on our experience during the past several years while managing numerous projects.

TEN PROJECT TIPS

1. Know your end customer (audience). Whether you are a consultant or an internal company champion, you should speak your customers' language, know their business, and understand their culture.

2. Know the project's objectives, scope, requirements, and commitments, and understand the return on investment (ROI) for the customer. Then think like a customer when you are faced with project issues.

3. Make sure the project team understands the business reasons for the project, as well as the project's commitments, requirements, scope, schedule, approach, and tasks.

4. Treat the customer as your partner. Engage your customer in the project, and create agreement on how key aspects of the project (communication, scope, change, and acceptance) will be managed. Then manage the project that way.

5. Tailor your approach for the needs of the project. Projects are not "one size fits all."

6. Set expectations early and often. Both customers and teams can take the hurdles better if they know they are coming.

7. Communicate, communicate, communicate—which often means "listen, listen, listen."

8. Trust and verify. Empower your team to be successful, and apply quality measures to ensure that they are. And learn from your mistakes.

9. Share risks with the customer. Everyone wants a successful project. By not sharing risks with the customer, you eliminate the one person who may be in the best position to mitigate them.

10. Yes, manage to the scope-schedule-cost triangle, and then think outside the triangle.

In addition to the standard tools and methodologies that are followed in project management, we have found that teaming, collaborating and communication play a major role in the success of a project. It is our experience that a primary barrier to project success is a lack of an effective approach to dashboard project execution and communications. We have described in the following text a disciplined approach for breaking through these barriers (see Exhibit 18.1).

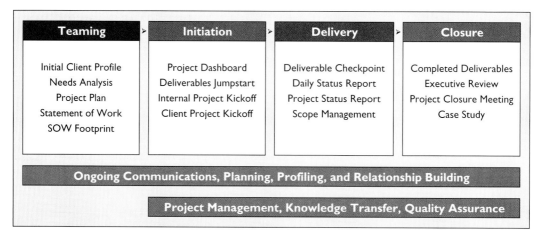

Teaming	Initiation	Delivery	Closure
Initial Client Profile	Project Dashboard	Deliverable Checkpoint	Completed Deliverables
Needs Analysis	Deliverables Jumpstart	Daily Status Report	Executive Review
Project Plan	Internal Project Kickoff	Project Status Report	Project Closure Meeting
Statement of Work	Client Project Kickoff	Scope Management	Case Study
SOW Footprint			

Ongoing Communications, Planning, Profiling, and Relationship Building

Project Management, Knowledge Transfer, Quality Assurance

EXHIBIT 18.1 Approach to Breaking the Dashboard Project Barriers

TEAMING

Teaming focuses on the complete understanding of the objectives of your audience, its priorities and requirements. Document and communicate your understanding of these issues throughout the teaming phase. Once enough information has been gathered, a Statement of Work and Project Plan are crafted, and a collaboration session takes place with the users to make final adjustments.

INITIATION

The initiation phase occurs once the users or stakeholders have signed off on the project. This phase of the Engagement Methodology formalizes the project kick-off procedures with the intent of getting all parties involved onto the same page prior to project execution. Preliminary project plans will be finalized during this phase as well as the review of project objectives, milestones, and success measures.

DELIVERY

The delivery phase of the Engagement Methodology encompasses the execution of the project itself. Leverage the appropriate components of the Delivery Methodology to produce the desired results of the project. Numerous communication and project management tools should be employed throughout this phase to ensure effective communications with all project team members and completion of deliverables consistent with the scope of the project.

CLOSURE

The focus of the closure phase is to turn over all final deliverables to the customer, to validate that they are well positioned to be successful with day-to-day operations of the solution, and to ensure that all expectations and critical success factors have been addressed. Document the project's success in the form of a Case Study.

chapter

Training and Deployment

19

The purpose of the User Training and Acceptance stage is:

- To provide the users (audience) with an opportunity to test and formally accept the dashboard application prior to Deployment. The tests should ensure that the dashboard application is functioning correctly, and that it provides the functionality agreed on in the specifications. A previously agreed-onset of acceptance criteria should be used to determine whether the customer should provide his or her sign-off.
- To ensure that all prerequisites for Deployment have been completed
- To ensure that the release will not have a detrimental impact on the current environment

Support documentation is also finalized during this stage—in particular the System Support Document but also any changes to the Technical Design and/or Implementation Plan required as a result of activities completed during this phase of the dashboard project.

KEY TASKS

The following is a list of key tasks that will help you prepare for user training and deployment of a dashboard application:

- Generate and structure all user support material with dashboard screenshots. If you have drill-down capabilities available in the dashboard, make sure those are highlighted.
- Have clear instructions for system access and authentication.

- Provide appropriate technical documentation for system support and technical support staff.
- Complete the User Acceptance Test (UAT) Plan.
- Complete the Deployment Plan.
- Complete the System Support Document.
- Schedule and prepare for the Acceptance meeting.
- Obtain approval to progress to Deployment.

TEMPLATES

User Acceptance Test Plan

What is the purpose of the template?

The UAT Plan should be used to ensure that all aspects of the dashboard application's functionality have been tested and the results recorded. The test plan should be based on information provided in the Business Requirements Document, together with any information identified subsequently.

Who is involved?

The Project Manager is responsible for agreement with the customer on the scope and format of the UAT. The Project Manager is also responsible for agreement with the customer on the acceptance criteria prior to commencing the UAT.

The Business Analyst is responsible for assisting the customer to create a detailed test plan.

The Test Coordinator is responsible for ensuring that a detailed test plan is available for test users that bugs identified during UAT are logged in the Test Log, and that testing takes place within agreed timeframes. Usually the Business Analyst could fill the role of Test Coordinator.

When should the template be completed?

The template should be started once the Business Requirements Document has been signed off, and should be completed by the closure of the Integration stage, with the exception of the UAT results.

System Support Document

What is the purpose of the template?

For the new dashboard application, a System Support Document should be created. This will hold basic information on the dashboard application for public consumption as well as links to other components to assist in the running and support of a system. The document should be created prior to a system's being rolled out to the production environment. If a System Support Document already exists (i.e., the project is delivering a change to an existing dashboard application), it should be updated to reflect the changes made through this project.

Who is involved?

The Project Manager, Application Specialist, Data Specialist, and Technical Architect contribute to this document.

When should the template be completed?

The template should be completed prior to the Acceptance Sign-Off.

Deployment Plan

What is the purpose of the template?

The template should detail the training requirements for the dashboard application and the plan for their execution, along with information on any specific rollout requirements including communication. It is also used to ensure that system infrastructure information for the release of the system to the production environment is captured and processed.

Who is involved?

The Project Manager will be responsible for ensuring the completion of the document. The participants in the actual production of the document will include the Business Analyst and other business area stakeholders.

When should the template be completed?

The template must be completed in most instances as part of the Acceptance stage (i.e., prior to the Deployment) to ensure that adequate time is available for training preparations and communication around the Deployment.

Acceptance Sign-Off

What is the purpose of the template?

Once the UAT Plan, System Support Document, and Deployment Plan have been signed off, the Project Manager should organize an acceptance sign-off and ask for approval to close the Acceptance Stage and move to Deployment. Based on the feedback received, the Project Manager should make a decision as to whether a meeting should be held to resolve any issues, noting where there is any ambiguity whatsoever as to whether a meeting should be held. Should a meeting be required, minutes should be recorded and linked to the acceptance sign-off.

Who is involved?

The acceptance sign off template is completed by the Project Manager, who is responsible for all communications.

When should the template be completed?

The completion of the acceptance sign off template and all associated actions should take place at the end of the Acceptance stage, once the UAT Plan System Support Document and Deployment Plan documents have been completed.

DASHBOARDS DEPLOYMENT

The aim of this stage is to successfully implement the project deliverables in the production environment, with minimal disruption to existing services, and to roll out the new dashboard functionality to the planned user community. The project manager has overall responsibility for the successful rollout and must ensure that the required resources are in place to complete this final stage of the project. A Finalized Technical Architecture Document and Implementation Plans are required for this stage.

The project manager must ensure that everyone is aware of the roles, the time frames, and the sequence of actions for the Deployment. We recommend a deployment meeting with all key resources. The project manager must also ensure that the users affected by the change are properly informed. Any service interruptions required for the Deployment should be agreed on with business partners and notified as Service Announcements to Production Management—this should be done at the outset of the stage. Typically, therefore, the Deployment Stage should begin at least two weeks before the planned implementation or roll-out date.

The project manager should carry out the deployment based on the agreed Implementation Plan. Rollout or deployment of dashboards will be supported as required by other project and information systems technical resources. In particular it is recommended that at least one member of the development team be available during the implementation.

The project manager should ensure the post-implementation checks are carried out by the Users. When these checks are completed, Production Management team will communicate to all end users that the system is available for use. If there are any problems with the deployment, Production Management will inform the project manager. The project manager will then coordinate an assessment of the situation and agree on the way forward with the key stakeholders. Production Management will communicate any impact on the service to the user community.

By the end of the stage, the project deliverables should be fully implemented and any problems dealt with. The stage is completed after formal acceptance of the deployment through the Deployment Sign-Off process.

KEY TASKS

The following is a list of key tasks that will serve as a checklist to ensure that training and deployment go smoothly:

- A service announcement should be issued to advise of any interruption to service, if any of the existing applications are affected due to this deployment.
- Deployment meetings should be held to ensure that all participants understand their role in the process.
- Training sessions and walkthroughs defined in the Training and Roll Out Plan should be carried out.
- A change freeze and the scope of its coverage should be agreed on by the project manager and customer or users. This will cover both project and support changes to the production environment during the period running up to the deployment.
- Deployment takes place in the production environment.

DEPLOYMENT SIGN-OFF

What is the purpose of the template?

Once the changes have been successfully deployed, the project manager should contact the key project stakeholders and ask for approval to close the Deployment stage. Based on the feedback received, the project manager should make a decision as to whether a meeting should be held to resolve any issues. Should a meeting be required, minutes should be recorded and linked to the Deployment Sign-Off Review.

Who is involved?

The Deployment Sign Off template is completed by the project manager.

When should the template be completed?

The completion of the Deployment Sign-Off template and all associated actions should take place at the end of the Deployment stage, once the implementation and associated documentation documents have been completed.

PART 4 SUMMARY AND READINESS CHECKLIST

To summarize, in this part we have discussed what an important role planning plays in a dashboard implementation project. Knowing the immediate requirements and discussing the long-term requirements at the very beginning of the project are critical so the most appropriate design and the most appropriate architecture are developed.

Also keep in mind that a dashboard development should not be conducted in silo and should be an iterative process, working closely with the end users. That way users can provide inputs along the way and receive the final product that they desired, thereby reducing the pains during User Acceptance Testing. Excessive involvement of users could pose some challenges in the progress of the project, as their requirements may keep changing. However, it is your job as a project lead or project manager to lay down strict guidelines to control scope creep.

Part 1 introduced you to dashboards and metrics, Part 2 discussed various architecture options that can drive a dashboard solution, and Part 3 gave you the tools you need to decide the type of dashboards you should be providing to your organization. The goal of this part was to give you insight and tips to successfully manage a dashboard project, based on lessons learned from real-world dashboard implementation projects.

You should now be ready to embark on the implementation of a dashboard project. The list that follows summarizes some of the key topics you have read in Part 4 of this book and lets you score your skills.

Scoring: Not sure = 1 point, Basic understanding = 2 points, Clear understanding = 3 points

	Score
☐ Importance of getting project sponsorship from leadership	
☐ Defining dashboard project goals and scope	
☐ Identifying team structure, roles, and members	
☐ Importance of communication plan	
☐ Importance of risk mitigation plan	
☐ Driving user interest and obtaining user support	
☐ Communicating business reasons for a dashboard implementation	
☐ Sufficient time allocation for planning and design	
☐ Monitoring dashboard usage	
☐ Understanding why post-deployment updates are important	
Total Score	

Place your total score in the right box in the following Scorecard:

Status	Points	Color	Your Score
Ready	21–30	●	
In Progress	15–20	○	
Not Ready	0–15	●	

APPENDICES

In the remainder of the book are five appendices. Each one covers an area that typically is of high importance in the process of selecting and implementing a dashboard solution. The appendices are meant to support the higher-level topics covered in the individual chapters, and they can be read in any particular order.

Software Selection Tips

S o far, this book has covered all the major areas that can help drive a successful dashboard implementation. This includes understanding the background and use of dashboards, data architecture, dashboard design, and project management. However, if you do not have the right dashboard technology to support your requirements, then at best your project might fall short on some objectives, or at worst it will fail. That is why we have included this appendix to help guide a software selection process.

The process of selecting a dashboard software package can involve anything from a sales department buying a $7,500 stand-alone dashboard solution on a vendor's website to a complex organization-wide decision with evaluation teams, request for proposal (RFP) documents, and a purchase that is aligned with a broad-based business intelligence initiative. The latter would likely take months, the dashboard software could have hundreds of users, and the price tag for software and services could be from $100,000 to several million dollars.

The remainder of this appendix will provide some guidelines and ideas that will be helpful to the team responsible for selecting the dashboard software in your organization.

TIPS BEFORE YOU START SOFTWARE EVALUATION AND SELECTION

Short-Term versus Long-Term Solution

One of the first questions you should ask yourself before the software evaluation starts is whether you are looking for a short- or a long-term solution. In some cases there is an imminent need for data visualization and a simple dashboard solution can be put in place quickly to take care of the users' needs. This would typically be an operational dashboard (see Chapter 4), and thus there would be no need to tie it to existing strategy or tactics and the level of complexity can be low. However, for an increasing number of institutions, a dashboard implementation is now a key element and the "crown jewel" of their long-term business intelligence (BI) strategy. Whatever technology is chosen needs to be compatible with all the other existing and planned BI tools and platforms. In this case, you want to ensure that your dashboard project is well announced and well coordinated with information technology (IT) and executive teams.

Getting Buy-In from the Rest of the Company

Once you and your team have decided that your organization needs a dashboard solution, it is generally a good idea to also make sure to "sell" the idea and benefits to all the parties (IT, finance, users, etc.) that will be affected by the decision. That way you reduce the chance that someone will stand up in the middle of the selection process and say something like "now why are we doing this again?" Or worse, if you are in the middle of the implementation and something does not go exactly as planned (as it often does with technology projects), you want to have the organization behind you to support work-arounds and time-schedule changes, and so on. The most typical case of lack of organizational support in software purchase decisions occurs in multi-location organizations, such as in a multinational company; corporate headquarters may decide to buy a BI software to roll it out everywhere, but does not do a good enough job in selling the idea to all the foreign subsidiaries. Such a situation will often result in lack of cooperation and enthusiasm for the solution once a global rollout starts.

Return-on-Investment and Cost-Benefit Analysis

To obtain a sign-off on a medium- to high-cost dashboard project from executive decision makers, you should expect to get questions about the expected return on investment (ROI) and the related costs and benefits. In other words, it is a good idea to do your homework in this area before you approach the chief executive officer (CEO) to get a software purchase approval. The nice thing about a dashboard solution is that it is highly visual; it is much easier to communicate to an executive how it will make someone's life easier, because most senior managers are often part of the target audience for such a solution.

Calculating the ROI for an IT project can be a very subjective task, given that it often is hard to put specific numbers on how much a company saves or the expected increase in revenue as a result of implementing dashboards. If your project is very large, you can probably justify soliciting outside help from a third-party consulting company to conduct this analysis. Of course, the whole idea with ROI and cost-benefit studies is for decision makers to have some tangible, estimated numbers to help them make an informed decision (such as "20% ROI per year" or "these ten benefits clearly outweigh the eight costs associated with this project").

Here is a simple example of an ROI analysis:

Estimated Investment:	
Dashboard software	$ 50,000
Other required software	$ 40,000
Annual maintenance fee	$ 18,000
Implementation costs	$110,000
TOTAL Investment	$218,000

Estimated Annual Return:	
Reduced need for reports	$ 20,000 (cost savings in annual report maintenance)
Reduced need for labor	$ 30,000 (self service vs. old solution)
Value-improved decisions	$ 90,000 (dashboards enable better decisions)
TOTAL Return	$140,000

ROI (based on an eight-year life of dashboard project): 55% return per year, and 441% ROI over an eight-year period. If these were the ROI numbers presented to an executive for a proposed dashboard project and the underlying assumptions and estimates were well grounded, chances are very good that the project would be approved.

Features and Flexibility

This is almost always the area where evaluation teams spend the most time during a software buying process. The key is to first describe the requirements (see the Business Requirements Document further on in this Appendix) of your organization and then match that against the features that the various software vendors have to offer. That matching process is, of course, one of the benefits of a structured buying process; vendors, after learning about your requirements, can then show your team how their software fulfills those requirements. In many cases, vendors will also be able to demonstrate features and flexibility that were not in your requirements, but once you become aware of them, you learn that they can be highly beneficial. However, make sure your required features are covered in discussions and demos, because vendors will always have their sales hats on and tend to focus on their slickest, most exciting functionality.

Compatibility with Existing Software

All application software, including dashboards, has dependencies on other software in order to function properly. Here are some examples of such dependencies that could exist or that your IT department would require in order for the dashboard software to be allowed:

- Data sources (enterprise resource planning (ERP) system, data warehouse, etc.):
  - File formats (text, comma separated, XML, Excel, etc.)
  - Data base platform (MS SQL, Oracle, IBM DB2, etc.)
  - Communication protocol (ODBC driver, Web Services, etc.)
- Add-ons (related value-added tools) to dashboard:
  - Microsoft Office integrations (Excel, PowerPoint, etc.)
  - Integration to other BI tools or modules from the same or another vendor
- Browser and portals:
  - Support of business portals (SharePoint, Websphere, etc.)
  - Support of web browsers (Explorer, Firefox, Netscape, etc.)

In summary, once you have mapped out the dashboard needs from an end-user (and strategic/tactical/operational) perspective, then make sure you involve IT and get their requirements and input.

Ease of Use

One of the major reasons many BI tools get heavily underutilized or even end up never being used is that they were too complex to maintain. In other words, busy users and administrators need tools that they can maintain with reasonable effort once the implementation has been completed. Vendors have made great strides in usability but there are still significant differences between various BI applications. In general, it still holds true that "there is no such thing as a free lunch." What this means is that the most advanced dashboard solutions with the most features and flexibility are generally also the technologies that require more set-up and more skill sets from the administrators and the end users. In some cases companies "dumb down" their dashboard application in the initial stages of deployment so as not to scare their users with too many options. Later, when a dashboard culture has developed, they open up more of the functionality.

The bottom line is that when the software selection committee is evaluating various dashboard solutions, they need to find that balance between ease of use and functionality, knowing that it typically is hard to get the best of both worlds in the same software.

Software Maturity

Around 2005, dashboards started to grow in popularity, and by 2008, they were something almost every executive in corporate and public-sector organizations were aware of and desired. There is no indication that this technology will not keep expanding onto executives' and managers' desktops for years to come. As usual, software vendors are becoming aware of the trend, and there are now numerous dashboard applications on the market. Some are from the large BI vendors (e.g., Microsoft, Oracle, IBM, and SAP), and others are from newcomers or smaller specialty vendors. The large vendors have integrated their dashboards with many of their other BI applications, platforms and portals, so they can offer customers an integrated suite of BI modules.

Regardless of the dashboard solutions you are considering, you need to look at the maturity of the application. If the product is early in its life cycle, your risk of bugs or certain features missing is higher then with a mature product, but you may gain some new, breakthrough benefits not offered by more mature solutions. However, if you are looking at a dashboard application that has been around for many years, it probably has more features, but it may lack support for newer platforms or related technologies. Either way, talk to some existing customers with needs similar to your own and ask what they like and do not like about the solution.

Due Diligence: Vendor

During 2007–08 a major consolidation in the BI industry occurred, and what used to be eight to ten fairly significant players suddenly narrowed down to four to five major companies with full-blown BI suites that consisted of a mix of homemade and acquired technologies. There are also a number of newer, smaller vendors coming into the market. Regardless, make sure you do the proper due diligence of a vendor (regardless of how much you liked its demo) before you make a final selection. You should check out such things as:

- Years in business
- Financials (are they making money or losing money? Cash flow?)
- Number of customers
- References
- Active product suites
- Planned new versions and related features
- Potential human resources issues (are key executives and employees staying around?)
- Plans to retire products or suites
- Number of consultants
- Availability and access methods for help desk and other support

- Availability and access methods (online or classroom) for training
- Availability and support for third-party add-on products
- Legal issues (pending lawsuits, etc.)
- Strategic vision and execution skills (is the vendor strategy aligned with your organization's current and future needs?)
- Expertise and special tools or templates for your industry
- Other customers in your industry
- Implementation capabilities (own or partner channel)
- Availability for software-as-a-service (hosted) from vendor or partner

The preceding list can be a good checklist to include in RFPs or during demos to remind you to ask all the key questions. It can help you pick a solid vendor and reduce the short- and long-term risks associated with the project immediately and after many years of using the technology.

Due Diligence: Implementation Partner

Working with a good implementation partner can be just as important as selecting a product and vendor. Even the strongest product can be implemented and configured poorly if performed by unskilled personnel. In short, you should do the same type of due diligence process for partner/consultant selection as you do for the vendor selection. Here are some tips on what to look for:

- Number of consultants trained on the vendor's product
- Experience with integration (ETL), data warehousing and online analytical processing (OLAP) if this is to be used in conjunction with the dashboards
- Number of successful implementations for each consultant
- Average implementation time for similar projects
- Hourly rate (and is it blended or different for type of consultant)
- Number of years consultants have worked with the product
- Does company offer skilled dashboard design consultants (regarding colors, layout, etc.) and data architecture consultants
- Special tools and/or intellectual property (dashboard templates, key performance indicators (KPIs), etc.) from similar projects that can be reused in your project
- Consultant experience with your industry (and related metrics)
- Financials
- Implementation methodology and related documents that will be used
- Consultant location (need to travel?)
- References

The due diligence of implementation partner candidates can be done face to face or via the phone or Web. For large projects, you should definitely have in-person meeting(s) with your chosen implementation partner prior to signing any agreements. This will help ensure a level of comfort and compatibility that does not always come through remote communication. Whatever promises are made, make sure you get them in writing. Also, for the project itself, you should get both a proposal and a related statement of work (which specifically lists rates, start dates, and deadlines, etc.). The more key facts you have in writing, the more likely it is that both parties will avoid conflicts or misunderstandings later.

SOFTWARE SELECTION PROCESS

Depending on the scope (large versus small) of your dashboard project, you can define the software selection process accordingly. In some cases, an organization may plan to use only a single operational dashboard in one department, which typically would mean that the cost and size of the project would be limited and hence the software and related selection process would need to be limited in scope and cost as well. In other cases, the implementation and rollout of dashboards are part of an overall corporate-wide, strategic performance management initiative, and the software selection process can be critical to ensure that the right technologies are chosen.

The following are a series of formal steps you can use to design your own organization's software selection process.

Step 1. Create a plan
- Clarify real need (what is the current pain, how can technology help, etc.).
- Identify an executive sponsor for the project and get approval.
- Map out how you want to run the evaluation process.
- Identify the selection team.
- Determine whether the dashboard software selection supports the current strategic vision, and if so, ensure there is mention of this and alignment.

Step 2. Decide next steps based on initial discovery. Based on Step 1, make decision on next steps:
- Move forward with the buying process.
- Upgrade existing software.
- Do nothing.

Step 3. Create a business requirement document (BRD) and/or a Request for Proposal (RFP). Assuming your decision in Step 2 was to move forward, a natural next step is to create a BRD and possibly an RFP.

The BRD is the most important document, as it will help educate vendors about things such as:

- Company background.
- Current pains.
- Technical environment (systems in place, database platforms, etc.,) and related requirements for dashboard project.
- Goals of dashboard project and initiatives it supports.
- Types of users and reporting relationships.
- Dashboard categories that are envisioned.

The RFP is a document that is sent out to a preselected group of vendors or resellers to formally request proposals based on the solutions they offer. Large RFPs are vastly unpopular among most vendors because they take a lot of time and cost to fill out, and sometimes RFPs favor a specific solution because they may be supplied by a specific vendor or consultancy in hope of putting their software in a favorable light. This situation usually does not gain any party, except the "insiders". In addition, it is almost impossible to list every possible feature you think you will ever need, and with RFP responses, in an attempt to look favorable, vendors will formulate their responses in ways that often do not clearly reflect the exact features. In other words, large RFPs often become massive, expensive exercises in verbal word juggling to make every answer to a question sound as good as possible. Instead of using large, detailed RFPs, we recommend that you keep the RFP short and to the point; instead spend your extra time and energy on a really solid BRD document. This will give vendors a firm understanding of your organization's needs, and they can use their time and energy as "business advisors" with years of software experience to recommend and show how their specific solution is going to solve your current and future needs. The RFP should contain:

- Short description of needs (it can refer to the BRD for detail).
- Your contact information.
- Request for key vendor/reseller information (years in business, customers, etc.).
- Description of the buying process (deadlines, rules, etc.).
- List of must-have features and platforms (to avoid spending any time on vendors that do not qualify).

Note: Many organizations use consulting companies to help them with the BRD and/or the RFP. If this extra expense is acceptable, having a fresh set of eyes and ears to provide an outside perspective to express needs and requirements can be advantageous.

Step 4. Create a vendor shortlist. Thanks to the Internet, today it is easy to find the key players in the dashboard software industry. Simply use your favorite search engine and put in search terms such as:

- "Dashboard vendor list."
- Dashboard and "vendor list."
- Dashboard and software.
- Dashboard and "business intelligence" and vendors.
- Dashboard and "performance management" and vendors.

In addition, there are, of course, printed publications and electronic newsletters and the like that from time to time will have buyers guides you can use.

The four largest players are IBM (acquired Cognos), Microsoft, Oracle (acquired Hyperion, Siebel), and SAP (acquired Business Objects), and there are a growing number of smaller players with good dashboard tools. With a quick search on the vendors' websites, you can typically see whether they support your core platform requirements and thus should go on your short list.

Step 5. Send out RFP and BRD. Do not forget to include instructions on the type of reply you prefer (hard copies, electronic, signed, etc.) and deadline.

Step 6. Receive vendor responses.

Step 7. Evaluate and short-list best vendors. Go through all the responses and pick the top two or three vendors that seem to have the best fit. Do phone interviews if necessary to help qualify or disqualify candidates.

Step 8. Send out replies and format for demos to chosen vendors. Provide the finalists with a choice of dates and times for demonstrations. We suggest a two-step process, where the first demonstration from each vendor is remote (demonstrations conducted via the Internet) and the second demonstration of the final candidate(s) is done in person. This is environmentally friendly and also provides a chance for vendors to adjust their demos so that the final one covers all the areas most interesting to the audience.

Step 9. Watch demos with the selection team and chose favorite vendor(s). Some companies like to use a highly structured demo format with scoring sheets on which each evaluation team member scores the different information and features being shown. At the same time, others may use more of a "gut feel" approach and a less structured demo in which vendors are encouraged to provide a natural flow based on what they have learned from studying your BRD and RFP.

Step 10. Request proposal with final pricing of software and services. Once your team has chosen its favorite vendor, make sure everyone is clear about:

- The exact software modules (e.g., dashboard, web portal, integration software, database) required.

- Number of and types of users.
- Project phases and related consulting and software requirements.

Step 11. Negotiate a contract and make a formal selection. You have now received the formal proposal from the finalist vendor, and if pricing, project scope, deadlines, and so forth are clearly defined and acceptable to both parties, provide a notice to the vendor that it is the chosen company.

Step 12. Sign the contract and make the purchase.

Note: You can receive a complimentary BI RFP template from the authors by sending an email to info@solverusa.com.

Installation

S imilar to most application servers, the most important thing in installation is the prerequisites. You should read through the prerequisites,
update the framework to the comparable version before you begin the
installation.

Exhibit B.1 and Exhibit B.2 are examples of Microsoft Performance Point
Monitoring Server requirements:

Item	Performance Point Monitoring Server Computer	File Share Server Computer	Performance Point Dashboard Designer Computer
Processor type	Minimum: 1x Pentium 4 Recommended: 2x dual-core 64-bit CPUs	Minimum: 1x Pentium 4 Recommended: 2x dual-core 64-bit CPUs	Minimum: 1x Pentium 3 Recommended: 1x dual-core 32-bit CPU (x86)
Processor speed	Minimum: 2.5 gigahertz (GHz) Recommended: 2.8 GHz	Minimum: 2.5 GHz Recommended: 2.8 GHz	Minimum: 1 GHz Recommended: 2.5 GHz
Available hard disk space	Minimum: 1 gigabyte (GB) Recommended: 5 GB 1 7,200 rpm hard disk drive	Minimum: 1 GB Recommended: 5 GB 1 7,200 rpm hard disk drive	Minimum: 512 mega-bytes (MB) Recommended: 2 GB
RAM	Minimum: 2 GB Recommended: 4 GB	Minimum: 2 GB Recommended: 4 GB	Minimum: 1.5 GB Recommended: 2 GB
Network interface	Minimum: 1,000BASE-T	Minimum: 1,000BASE-T	Minimum: 1,000BASE-T

EXHIBIT B.1 Monitoring Server Hardware Prerequisites

Prerequisite	Required For Installing
Microsoft SQL Server 2005 database software (Standard or Enterprise Edition)	Monitoring System Database
Internet Information Services (IIS) 6.0 Internet Information Services (IIS) 5.1 (for Windows XP) Microsoft ASP.NET 2.0 The Microsoft .NET Framework version 2.0.50727 IIS 6.0 worker process isolation mode Microsoft ASP.NET 2.0 registration with IIS ASP.NET 2.0 Web Service Extension in IIS	Monitoring Server IIS component
Report Designer Plug-In for the Microsoft Visual Studio 2005 development system.	Monitoring Plug-in for Report Designer
Windows SharePoint Services 3.0 Microsoft Office SharePoint Server 2007	Dashboard Viewer for SharePoint Services
Microsoft SQL Server 2005 Reporting Services	Scorecard Viewer for Reporting Services
SQL Server Native Client 9.0 SP2 (http://go.microsoft.com/fwlink/?LinkID=87078)	Monitoring System Database Monitoring Server

EXHIBIT B.2 Monitoring Server Software Prerequisites

The installation process itself differs from system to system, but all are pretty self-explanatory. Reading through the system document would be the key to a successful installation.

Hardware Recommendations

A business intelligence (BI) implementation normally requires four parts:

1. Relational database server
2. OLAP database server
3. Web server
4. Dashboard or BI server

RELATIONAL DATABASE SERVER

The role of a relational database server in relation to BI is mostly that of staging database and system database. The hardware consumption of the staging database server greatly depends on how much of the source online transaction processing (OLTP) system data is to be replicated, the transformation rules, and the LAN/WAN pipe.

Hard disk—wise, you should allocate at least three times of your OLTP database size as your hard disk requirement, because of the staging transformation. Keep in mind, every stage of your transformation can be used for reporting down the road; therefore, keeping the transformation aligned with the metadata would be ideal.

CPU consumption depends mostly on the complexity and the volume of the transformation. Consider that you are changing the account codes from "100-000-102" to "100-001-200." Making this change for 1,000 records certainly is much faster than for 1,000,000 records. Additionally, writing correct scripts would help in resource consumption. Refer to the ETL section in Chapter 9 for economical scripting tips. Generally, the more CPUs are in the system, the more processes we can run simultaneously, which helps the load time. We refer to this as "parallel load." Some BI/ETL tools can take advantage of the multi-CPUs, some cannot. See the system documents to determine whether you can benefit from such a setting. Aside from that, the faster the CPU clock speed, the faster the process.

Memory size also depends on the complexity and the volume of the transformation. Keep in mind, this is for a data warehouse process, not for a transactional process. The normal hardware specification for an OLTP system is not applicable in the present case. We are processing data at a whole data-set level, not at a transactional level. This means we need sufficient memory and "temp" database space to store the interim information.

OLAP DATABASE SERVER

One thing that people tend to forget is the amount of resources the analytics server needs. Many people think this is similar to the traditional relational database server, but in fact it is not. After all, this server performs most of the heavy lifting in calculations. It certainly needs more resources to do the work.

Oracle Essbase, one of the long-term online analytical processing (OLAP) servers, is one example. Essbase, as an application server, does not require a large amount of resources in itself. However, the produced OLAP databases may be hundreds of gigabytes in size. During the data load and calculation time, it consumes all the memory available to perform its task. That is what produces the preaggregated result and enhances the query performance.

Microsoft SQL Server Analytics Service is similar to Essbase in regard to resource consumption during load and calculation time. However, it does not take up nearly as much hard drive space because the database is scripted in XML.

It is common to designate the fastest CPUs with most memory machine to the analytics server. Quad-Core CPUs are common, depending on the scale of the project; 16 to 32 GB RAM is also common.

WEB SERVER

The payload of a web server is what determines the user interface performance. It mainly has to do with the number of concurrent users. In the case of BI processing, the web server also hosts the Servlets that are embedded in the dashboards. It caches queried results for end users. So, while the number of concurrent sessions would determine the system consumption, the "similarity" of the dashboard queries also makes a big difference. This leads to the way we design dashboards. When we design dashboards, we should already have in mind which queries are likely to be triggered by the interactions. The more we can reuse the cached data set on the web server, the faster the information is delivered to end users. Similarly, the less time we spend to reconnect to the data warehouse, the faster we deliver information to the users.

DASHBOARD SERVER

A dashboard server, or a BI Server, basically keeps the dashboard objects and user access rights to these objects. The resource consumption is fairly minimal. Most objects are stored as some kind of scripts (e.g., Java, C#, XML, etc.). The performance of a dashboard server depends on the underlying scripts and the number of concurrent user sessions. Using economical query script against the data warehouse can help conserve the system resource consumption.

Taking the Microsoft Performance Point Server as an example, the baseline configuration recommends[1] the following:

- SQL Server Analysis Services:
  - 2-socket Quad-Core 3.0 GHz processors or better
  - 16 GB RAM
  - (2) 72 GB 10K RPM drives in a RAID-1 Array
  - (6) 146 GB 10K RPM drives in a RAID-10 Array
  - 1,000 Mbps Network Interface
- SharePoint Services 3.0 and Monitoring Server:
  - 2-socket Quad-Core 3.0 Ghz processors or better
  - 16 GB RAM
  - (2) 72 GB 10K RPM drives in a RAID-1 Array
  - (6) 146 10K RPM drives in a RAID-10 Array
  - 1,000 Mbps Network Interface
- SQL Server 2005 DB, SSIS and SSRS:
  - 4-socket Quad-Core 3.0 GHz processors or better
  - 32 GB RAM
  - (2) 72 GB 10K RPM drives in a RAID-1 Array
  - (6) 146 GB 10K RPM drives in a RAID-10 Array
  - 1000 Mbps Network Interface

NOTE

1. For more information, see "Best practices for deploying Microsoft Office Performance Point solutions on HP Servers" on Hewlett-Packard web site.

Security Authentication Techniques

The security scheme being used has a major effect not only on user access but on dashboard performance. A well-constructed chain of authentication requires less time to validate credentials and thus improves data delivery.

In the infrastructure breakdown, we need to streamline the authentication all the way from database server, through the online analytical processing (OLAP) server, through the web server and the business intelligence (BI) server, and finally to delivery to end users' workstations. It is certainly a much easier task if all servers and workstations are on the same operating system platform. In the Microsoft world, every product is authenticated via Windows Active Directory, offering streamlined authentication. In the non-Microsoft world, different operating systems have different security schemes. Generally, there are lightweight directory access protocol (LDAP) servers that manage the cross-authentication process.

To complement the Windows Active Directory or LDAP, we can also configure web servers to accept secure sockets layer (SSL). SSL is a communication protocol that requires encrypted certificates to access the website. This enforces user ID authentication at the entry point.

Kerberos is another layer of security protocol. Kerberos is a network authentication protocol, designed to provide stronger authentication for client/server applications by using secret-key cryptography. Kerberos allows the correct credentials to be passed from one application server to another, across the network. When implementing a multi-server BI environment, Kerberos authentication is absolutely critical.

From the OLAP standpoint, we may use Multi-dimensional Scripts to set securities. The user ID would have rights to certain "slices" of the cube. Similarly, many relational database management systems (RDBMS) offer column-based as well as row-based securities to restrict user access to certain data sets.

Metrics and Key Performance Indicator Examples

In this appendix we have listed a large number of metrics and key performance indicators (KPIs) with the goal of providing ideas and possibly fully usable items for use in your dashboards and scorecards. In the first section, we have organized all the content by departmental function; in the second section, it is organized by industry (based on the U.S. Government's, Standard Industrial Classification system).

METRICS AND KPIS BY DEPARTMENTAL FUNCTION

In the following section you will find a large number of sample metrics and key performance indicators (KPIs) for common departments:

- Customer service
- Finance
- Human resources
- Information technology
- Marketing
- Sales

Customer Service

Agent's full-time employees (FTEs) as percentage of total call center FTEs

Answering percentage (number of sales calls answered/total number of sales calls offered)

Average after-call work time

Average number of calls/service request per handler

Average queue time of incoming phone calls

Cost per minute of handle time

Costs of operating call center/service desk

E-mail backlog

Field service technician utilization

Hitrate (products sold compared to total received sales calls)

Inbound abandon rate

Inbound agent dialed calls

Inbound availability rate

Inbound average talk time

Inbound average wrap time

Inbound call center leads created

Inbound call center opportunities created

Inbound calls handled

Inbound calls handled per agent hour

Inbound service level

Number of complaints

Percentage of customer service requests answered in given timeframe

Percentage of calls transferred

Total calling time per day/week/month

Finance

Accounting costs

Accounts payable turnover

Accounts receivable collection period

Accounts receivable turnover

Actual expenses

Amount due (per customer)

Average customer receivable

Average monetary value of invoices outstanding

Average monetary value of overdue invoices

Average number of trackbacks per post

Budget variance for each key metric

Budgeted expenses

Capital expenditures

Cash conversion cycle (CCC)

Cash flow return on investments (CFROI)

Cost of goods sold (COGS)

Cash dividends paid

Cost per pay slip issued

Creditor days

Current receivables

Cumulative annual growth rate (CAGR)

Cycle time for expense reimbursements

Cycle time to process payroll

Cycle time to resolve an invoice error

Cycle time to resolve payroll errors

Days payable

Debtor days

Direct costs

Discounted cash flow

Earnings before interest and taxes (EBIT)

Earnings before interest, taxes, depreciation (EBITDA)

Economic value added (EVA)

Employee available time

Employee scheduled time

Employee work center loading

Enterprise value/takeover value

Expense account credit transactions

Expense account debit transactions

Expense account transactions

Fixed costs

Gross profit

Gross profit margin

Indirect costs

Inventory turnover

Inventory value

Invoice processing costs

Internal rate of return (IRR)

Market share gain comparison percentage

Net change in cash

Net income

Net present value (NPV)

Number of invoices outstanding

Number of unapplied receipts

Number of past-due loans

Open receivables

Open receivables amount (per customer)

Operating leverage

Past-due receivables

Payables turnover

Payment errors as a percentage of total payroll disbursement

Percentage accuracy of financial reports

Percentage of bad debts against invoiced revenue

Percentage of electronic invoices

Percentage in dispute (per customer)

Percentage of invoices being queried

Percentage of invoices requiring special payment

Percentage of low-value invoices

Percentage of open receivables (per customer)

Percentage of payable invoices without purchase order

Percentage of service requests posted via web (self-help)

Perfect order measure

Quick ratio

Receivables

Receivables turnover

Return on capital employed (ROCE)

Sales growth

Share price

Systems cost of payroll process as a percentage of total payroll cost

Total payables

Total energy used per unit of production

Total receivables

Total sales

Unapplied receipts

Variable costs

Weighted days delinquent sales outstanding

Weighted days delinquent sales outstanding (per customer)

Weighted terms outstanding

Weighted terms outstanding (per customer)

Human Resources

Actual versus budgeted cost of hire

Annualized voluntary employee turnover rate

Annualized voluntary turnover rate

Average headcount of employees each human resources (HR) employee working is caring for

Average interviewing costs

Average length of placement in months for the manager

Average length of service of all current employees

Average length of service of all employees who have separated

Average months placement

Average number of training hours per employee

Average number of vacation days per employee

Average performance scores of departing employees

Average retirement age

Average salary

Average salary for all employees reporting to the selected manager

Average sourcing cost per hire

Average time employees are in same job/function

Average time to competence

Average time to update employee records

Average training costs per employee

Compensation cost as a percentage of revenue

Contingent workers

Employee satisfaction with training

End placements

Female-to-male ratio

Full-time employees (FTEs) per human resources (HR) department FTE

Headcount of contingent workers for the manager

HR average years of service (incumbents)

HR average years of service (terminations)

HR department cost per FTE

HR headcount: Actual

HR headcount: Available

HR to employee staff ratio

Job vacancies as a percentage of all positions

New hire quality

Time to fill

Hiring manager satisfaction

Cost per hire

Staffing efficiency

Internal, external, and total headcount recruiting costs and ratios

Number of end placements made in the reporting period for the manager

Part-time employees as a percentage of total employees

Percentage of employees receiving regular performance reviews

Percentage of employees that are near or at max for their vacation balances

Percentage of HR budget spent on training

Percentage of new hire retention

Ratio of internal versus external training

Ratio of standard level wage to local minimum wage

Return on investment (ROI) of training

Total overtime hours as a percentage of all work hours

Training penetration rate (percentage of employees completing a course compared to all FTEs)

Workforce stability

Information Technology

Account create success

Account termination success

Active directory performance index

Alert-to-ticket ratio

Average data center availability

Call center PBX availability

Campus PBX availability

Customer connection effectiveness

Data center capacity consumed

E-mail client availability

Exchange server availability

Incidents from change

Internet proxy performance

Network availability: High availability sites

Network availability: Standard sites

Network manageability index

No problem found/duplicate tickets

Percentage of branch office backup success

Percentage of circuits exceeding target utilization

Percentage of IT managed servers patched at deadline

Percentage of production servers meeting software configuration standards

Percentage of security update restarts within maintenance window

Percentage successful remote access server (RAS) connections

Phone answer service level

Priority 1 and priority 2 network incidents meeting SLA

Product adoption status and compliance

Restore success rate

Server growth rate

Server manageability index

Service desk client satisfaction: Percentage dissatisfied

Service desk tier 1 resolution rate

Service desk time to escalate

Service desk time to resolve

Storage utility service availability

Storage utility utilization

Virtual machine provisioning interval

Virtual server utility availability

Web server availability

Marketing

Ad click-through ratio (CTR)

Average response rates of campaigns

Brand awareness percentage

Brand consideration

Brand credibility

Brand strength

Column inches of media coverage

Consumer awareness

Contact rate (number of contacts effectively contacted/number of contacts in the target list)

Cost per converted lead

Cost per lead

Cost per mille (CPM)

Delivery of materials

Effective reach

Gross rating point (GRP)

Growth sustainability rate of brand

Leads generated

Marketing budget awareness-demand ratio

Marketing budget ratio (MBR)

Number of article placements in trade magazines

Number of client visits

Number of product focus groups conducted

Number of customer satisfaction surveys administered

Number of placements in trade magazines

Number of trade shows attended/participated in

Website hits/click-throughs/leads generated

Percentage of customers willing to promote your product/service

Q score (a way to measure the familiarity and appeal of a brand, etc.)

Response rate

Return on investment (ROI) of brand

Return on marketing investment (ROMI)

Revenue generation capabilities of brand

Staying in budget

Target rating point

Total cost of customer acquisition

Transaction value of brand

Website hits

Sales

Actual calls

Actual sales value versus initial bid

Age of sales forecast

Average administrative time per sales person

Average deal size

Average number of activities (calls, meetings, etc.) to close a deal

Average price discount per product

Average price discount per sales person

Average revenue per product

Call quota

Closed sales

Closing ratio

Customer acquisitions costs as a percentage of sales value

Customer churn ratio

Customer loyalty

Customer purchase frequency

Customer satisfaction

Frequency of sales transactions

Gross margin per product

Gross margin per sales person

New sales person ramp-up time

Number of certified partners

Number of deals per partner

Number of sales orders by FTE

Number of sales people meeting their quota

Number of units sold per day/week/month/quarter/year

Partner churn ratio

Partner profit margin

Percentage of converted opportunities

Percentage of online sales revenue

Percentage of sales due to launched product/services

Percentage of sales representatives to achieve quota

Percentage of sales revenue via partner channel

Pipeline by sales stage

Qualified leads

Qualified opportunities

Revenue per sales person

Sales capacity

Sales cycle time

Sales per department

Sales person turnover

Sales quota

Time utilization

Unweighted sum of deal size in sales pipeline

Value of sales lost

Win/loss ratio percentage

METRICS AND KPIS BY INDUSTRY

In the following section you will find a large number of sample metrics and KPIs for all the 21 major industry categorizations (see the following list):

- Accommodation and food services
- Administrative and support and waste management and remediation services
- Agriculture, forestry, fishing, and hunting
- Arts, entertainment, and recreation
- Construction
- Educational services
- Finance and insurance
- Health care and social assistance
- Information
- Management of companies and enterprises
- Manufacturing
- Mining
- Other services (except public administration)
- Professional, scientific, and technical services
- Public administration
- Real estate and rental and leasing
- Retail trade
- Transportation and warehousing
- Utilities
- Wholesale trade

Accommodation and Food Services

General

Average revenue per guest

Average revenue per table

Complaints per head

Complaints per order

Labor cost per guest

Labor cost per table

Minutes per table turn

Profit per table

Bar and Cellar Management

Average profit percentage on sales

Carrying cost of stock

Gross profit on sales

Sales and stocktaking discrepancies

Sales per head

Stock turnover

Stock value

Front of House and Restaurant Management

Customer satisfaction

Front of house labor hours

Food, dessert, and beverage sales per head

Front of house labor percentage

Linen costs

Number of customers

Revenue per available seat hour (RevPASH)

Seating efficiency

Strike rate: Number of diners over number of occupying guests

Total sales per head: Total sales divided by the number of customers.

Kitchen Management

Food cost percentage: Food cost over food sales

Food costs per head

Kitchen labor percentage: Kitchen labor cost over food sales

Kitchen labor hours: Over sales

Kitchen linen costs

Percentage of sales per selling items

Stock value

Total food costs

Management of Finance and Administration

Cash position at bank

Administration labor costs

Computer and technology efficiency (percentage of downtime, POS accuracy, staff equipment literacy rate)

Taxes owed

Return on investment

Sales and costs: Actual versus budget as a percentage

Stocktaking discrepancies per department

Total (short term) accounts due

Total accounts payable

Sales and Marketing plus Function Management

Booking forecast: Future *x* weeks/months, special holidays

Number of function inquiries, percentage of campaign cost against functions

Marketing and advertising costs and cost per response as ratio

Number of customers

Press mentions

Campaign response rate

Sales inquiry conversion rate: The number of inquiries that turn into actual sales

Sales per head (across all areas)

Repeat visits, especially by top 100 or 200 customers

Staffing

Average hourly pay

Average length of employment

Profit/markup on function labor charge-out (caterers)

Labor turnover (number of new staff in any one week or month)

Sick days taken (as a percentage of total available working days)

Total labor cost percentage

Total labor hours per each section

Wage cost percentage: Wage costs as a percentage of sales.

Administrative and Support and Waste Management and Remediation Services

General

(Electronics) Sub-sector indicators: For printed circuit board (PCB), semiconductor, and cathode ray tube (CRT) manufacture

Chemical emission rate per facility

Compliance with water license conditions

Cost per load

Demolition recovery index and new build recovery index

Discharge efficiency

Energy indicators

Facility saturation rate

Percentage of hazardous material over total waste

Percentage of reusable/recycled material

Percentage of sample failure

Percentage of total waste diverted from landfill and other disposal options

Percentage of waste recycled off site

Percentage of wastewater treatment works meeting license conditions

Percentage of waste reused off site

Percentage of waste reused on site

Pollution indicators (emissions to air, effluent, solid waste)

Potable water consumption

Renewable energy consumption

Segregation rate

Site level indicators of resource efficiency

Surface runoff efficiency

Total recycled content by material value

Transport time efficiency

Waste cost per carriage way or pipeline length

Waste cost per project as percentage

Waste cost per project footprint

Waste cost per square meter floor area

Waste generation (tonnage) per project

Waste generation (tonnage) per square meter/foot

Waste generation (volume) per project

Waste generation (volume) per square meter/foot

Wastewater discharge quality

Emissions to Air

Acid rain, eutrophication, and smog precursors

Dust and particles

Greenhouse gases

Metal emissions to air

Ozone depleting substances

Volatile organic compounds

Emissions to Water

Nutrients and organic pollutants

Metal emissions to water

Emissions to Land

Acids and organic pollutants

Metal emissions to land

Pesticides and fertilizers

Radioactive waste

Waste (landfill, incinerated, and recycled)

Resource Use

Aggregates

Agriculture

Coal

Forestry

Metals

Minerals

Natural gas

Oil

Water use and abstraction

Growth or reduction of preceding KPIs

Agriculture, Forestry, Fishing, and Hunting

21-day weight per litter

Amount of trees planted versus actual planted by percentage

Average number of harvest per year

Carbon dioxide per square mile

Cost per wildfire

Customer satisfaction level (CSAT)

Domestic demands versus supply

Dust and particles per square mile

Establishment's occupancy

Establishment's rate

Export rate

Import rate

Increase or decrease in number of complaints over time

Increase or decrease in number of hunting applications over time

Industry employment source and turnover rate

Industry gross product

Industry revenue

Landslides caused by wildfires

Number of wildfires

Percentage of increase in rod license

Percentage of increase or decrease in fish count (in relation to ecological effects)

Percentage of hazards minimized within x hours of notification

Percentage of live birth (per each animal group)

Percentage of natural resources accessed

Percentage of natural resources sustained

Total wages

Wean per litter

Weight per litter at birth

Arts, Entertainment, and Recreation

Institutional KPIs

Album publication over total submission

Average ticket price per season

Cost per broadcast hour

Cost per performing night

Cost per production hour

Cost per viewer/listener

Donation percentage of total revenue

Donation increase/decrease over time

Employer satisfaction rate

Employment rate

Gallery showing over total submission

Graduation rate

Increase/decrease number of performance nights per year

Market share

Net surplus percentage

Number of kindergarten through 12th grade school tours per year

Occupancy rate

Percentage of broadcast hours by genre

Percentage of national content (broadcasting organizations)

Percentage of overhead against total expenditure

Profit percentage

Ratio of amateur versus professional performers

Revenue

Seating efficiency

Special/guest appearance cost per revenue

Telcvision show rating

Utilization rate (recording studio, concert hall, art studio)

Viewer/listeners for each medium as a percentage of total population

Personal KPI

Number of awards

Number of gallery showings per year

Number of public appearances per year

Number of published recordings

Number of renowned awards (e.g., Billboard, Oscar, etc.)

Ratio of won competitions over participated

Construction

Number of accidents

Number of accidents per supplier

Actual working days versus Available working days

Cash balance: Actual versus baseline

Change orders: Clients

Change orders: Project manager

Client satisfaction: Client-specified criteria

Client satisfaction product: Standard criteria

Client satisfaction service: Standard criteria

Cost for construction

Cost predictability: Construction

Cost predictability: Construction (client change orders)

Cost predictability; Construction (project leader change orders)

Cost predictability: Design

Cost predictability: Design and construction

Cost to rectify defects

Customer satisfaction level

Day-to-day project completion ratio: Actual versus baseline

Fatalities

Interest cover (company)

Labor cost: Actual versus baseline

Labor cost over project timeline

Liability ratio (over asset) on current versus completion comparison

Number of defects

Outstanding money (project)

Percentage of equipment downtime

Percentage of labor downtime

Percentage of backlogs over project timeline

Percentage of unapproved change orders

Productivity (company)

Profit margin: Actual versus baseline

Profit margin over project timeline

Profit predictability (project)

Profitability (company)

Quality issues at available for use

Quality issues at end of defect rectification period

Ratio of value added (company)

Repeat business (company)

Reportable accidents (including fatalities)

Reportable accidents (non-fatal)

Return on capital employed (company)

Return on investment (client)

Return on value added (company)

Time for construction

Time predictability: Construction

Time predictability: Construction (client change orders)

Time predictability: Construction (project leader change orders)

Time predictability: Design

Time predictability: Design and construction

Time taken to reach final account (project)

Time to rectify defects

Educational Services

Administrative expenses as a percentage of educational and general expenditures

Admission test scores for entering students

Annual student survey: Two-year comparison in five key areas

Attrition rate of online courses

Average course experience

Average daily attendance

Average daily participation percentages

Average endowment distribution by student

Average net academic cost and average percent discount

Average percentage consistently absent

Average student credit hours taught by tenure/tenure track faculty by college

Average tenure or tenure track faculty salaries by college compared to peer benchmarks

Average undergraduate student credit load

Average unmet free application for federal student aid Financial Need (FASFA) by student and graduating student debt average

Choice into district: Number of students

Choice out of district: Number of students

Class attendance

Classroom and laboratory utilization

Comparison of most recent graduating high school classes to diversity of new 18- and 19-year-old students who enroll in the following fall term

Continuation rates of college students

Cost per graduate

Cost per meal (CPM)

Degrees awarded: Baccalaureate, masters, doctoral

Development expenditures as a percentage of total external income

Distance learning enrollment

Distance learning number of degree programs

Dollar value of restricted research expenditures

Dollar value of total external research grant applications and expenditures

Endowment value per student

Expenditures per student

Fewer students classified as needing special education services

Four-year graduation rate for community college transfer students with 30+ hours

Freshman retention rate by ethnic group and by financial aid category

Fund balance at x % of yearly expenditures

Graduate/professional degrees in high demand fields

Home school students registered: Number of students

Increase of percentage of school-age students with disabilities participating in occupational education program

Increase of percentage of school-age students with disabilities receiving special education services in general class placements

Increase of percentage of preschool students with disabilities receiving special education services in settings which include nondisabled children

Increase of percentage of school-age students with disabilities receiving services in general education buildings

Institutional debt per student

Instructional expenses per student

International student load

International student headcount and percentage of FTE

Licensure exam pass rates

Licensure exam pass rates in program x

Master's-level five-year and doctoral ten-year graduation rate

Masters and doctoral graduates employed in state x compared to other state x graduates

National ranking of baccalaureate, masters, and doctoral degrees awarded to minority students

Nationally ranked programs

NCAA team sports athletics total wins

Noninstructional FTE per student FTSE, or noninstructional FTE to instructional FTE ratio

NSSE results in quality of student advising, entire educational experience, would attend again, overall satisfaction

Number of degrees awarded

Number of students per teacher

Number of total budgeted tenure/tenure track faculty positions

Number of vocational degrees awarded

Percentage of academic staff with a doctorate

Percentage of full-time faculty who are women or ethnic minorities or have terminal degrees

Percentage of course requests satisfied by semester

Percentage of degree-seeking new transfers (of total enrollment)

Percentage of first year class in top 10% and top 25% of HS graduating class

Percentage of first year students requiring developmental education and successful completion percentage of developmental education

Percentage of graduating seniors from area high schools from most recent academic year that enroll in following fall term

Percentage of new students, ages 18 to 19, who need developmental education based on their test scores

Percentage of tenure/tenure track faculty holding grants by college

Percentage of total positions endowed

Percentage of undergraduates receiving baccalaureate degrees with eight SCH or fewer above minimum requirement, number qualifying for state mandated rebate, and number requesting and receiving their rebate

Postdoctoral fellows

Program expenditures as a percentage of budgets

Research rankings national and state

Retention rates of students in vocational courses

SCH taught by tenure/tenure track faculty vs. non-tenure/tenure track faculty by college

Six-year graduation rate and combined graduation/persistence rate

Student services expenditures per student FTSE

Students per faculty

Successful course completion

System-wide reduction in energy use over ten years

Technology transfer: new invention disclosures, patents issues, licenses and options executed, gross revenue from intellectual property

Time to a baccalaureate degree by area of study

Total budgeted endowed professorships and chairs

Total degree seeking new transfers

Total external gifts by alumni: Number and amount

Total external gifts by corporations: Number and amount

Total external gifts by foundations: Number and amount

Total external gifts by individuals: Number and amount

Total new transfer students

Total operating expenditures per student FTE

Total professorships and chairs positions filled

Total state appropriations per FTE student and tuition and fees per FTE student in constant dollars

Total state appropriations per FTE student compared to peers

Total stipend support for graduate students

Transportation costs per pupil

Tuition and mandatory fees compared to peers

Undergraduate classes with fewer than 30 students

Undergraduate degrees in high demand fields

Undergraduate financial aid awards

Undergraduates per professional academic advisor by college

Unrestricted reserves as percentage of operating budget

University students studying abroad headcount

Yellow bus on-time performance

Finance and Insurance

Finance

Accounting costs

Accounts payable

Accounts payable turnover

Asset turnover rate

Average sum deposited in new deposit accounts

Average value of past due loans

Cash conversion cycle (CCC)

Cash dividends paid

Cash flow return on investments (CFROI)

Common stock equity

Cost of goods sold (COGS)

Cost per hour per lawyer (in-house)

Creditor days

Cumulative annual growth rate (CAGR)

Cycle time to perform periodic close

Cycle time to resolve an invoice error

Days payable

Debt-to-asset ratio

Debtor days

Direct costs

Earnings per share (EPS)

EBIT

EBITDA

Economic value added

Enterprise value/takeover value

Fixed costs

Gross margin on managed assets

Gross profit

Gross profit margin

Indirect costs

Interest expense

Interest on net worth

Invoicing processing costs

Labor and management cost

Labor and management earnings

Legal staff per size of revenue

Long-term debt

Marginal costs

Market share

Net change in cash

Net interest margin

Net new money

Net profit

Net profit margin

Number of budget deviations

Number of invoices outstanding

Number of past due loans

Operating income

Operating leverage

Operating margin

Operating profit margin

Other current liabilities

Other noncurrent liabilities

Percentage of accuracy of periodic financial reports

Percentage of effectiveness in payables management

Percentage of budget deviation relative to total budget

Percentage of electronic invoices

Percentage of financial reports issued on time

Percentage of invoices requiring special payment

Percentage of invoices under query

Percentage of legal budget spent outside

Percentage of low-value invoices

Percentage of payable invoices without purchase order

Preferred stock equity

Product turnover ratio

Profit

Profit loss due to theft

Profit margin

Profit per product

Quick ratio

Rate of return on assets

Rate of return on equity

Return on assets

Return on capital employed (ROCE)

Return on investment (ROI)

Return to equity

Revenue

Revenue per employee

Sales per share

Same store sales

Selling general and administrative (SG&A) expenses

Share price

Shares outstanding

Sharpe ratio

Short-term debt

Sortino ratio

Systems cost of payroll process as a percentage of total payroll cost

Tier 1 capital

Total assets

Total current liabilities

Total equity

Total legal spending as a percentage of revenue

Total liabilities

Total of uninvested funds

Total quantity of new deposit accounts

Total sum deposited in new deposit accounts

Total value of past due loans

Variable costs

Insurance

Average insurance policy size

Claims

Combined cost and claims ratio

Combined ratio

Current premium versus loss

Earned premium

Expense ratio

Expenses

Exposure

Loss adjustment expenses (LAE)

Loss ratio

Number of days open of insurance claims

Number of new insurance policies

Previous premium versus loss

Underwriting speed of insurances

Written premium

Health Care and Social Assistance

Accounts receivable

Accounts payable and accrued expenses

Admissions in-patient

Average length of stay (ALOS)

ALOS for top ten diagnoses

Assets in current period

Assets in prior period

Average age of plant

Average age of workforce

Average daily and monthly census

Average hourly rate

Average length of stay

Average payment period (days)

Average time to fill positions

Backorder percentage

Bad debt as percentage of net revenue

Bottleneck areas

Break even

Capital expenditure growth rate

Case mix index

Cash and equivalents

Cash collected versus target

Cash on hand (days)

Communication effectiveness

Contract negotiation schedule

Cost per discharge

Current asset turnover

Current ratio

Days in accounts receivable

Debt service coverage ratio

Depreciation funds

Depreciation rate

Discharge process time

Discharges in-patient

Discounts trends, revenue, and margin by payer class

Due to third parties

Education funds

Emergency visits outpatient

Encounters outpatient

Equity financing

Errors related to procedure/treatment or test

Events, number of events by type and department

Expenses per physician FTE

Fixed asset turnover

Free operating cash flow to assets

Free operating cash flow to revenue

FTE per occupied bed

FTEs per adjusted occupied bed

Growth rate on equity

Hazardous materials usage

Informed about delays

Inventory ratio

Inventory turnover

Investments at market value

Long-term debt

Long-term investments

Maintained bed occupancy

Mean wait time in emergency department (ED) for hospital bed

Medication errors, number of errors per 1,000 treatments

Medication errors, number of errors per month/year

Month to date (MTD) bad debt

MTD cash collected

MTD revenue

Net assets

Net income

Net income to patient revenue

Net revenue

Non-operating gains

Number of new hires per day

Nurse turnover rate

Nurse vacancy rate

Nurses attention to needs

Operating income

Operating profit margin

Operating revenues

Other liabilities

Outside labor as a percentage of total

Over or under consumption of service lines by payer types

Overtime costs

Paid time off costs at business unit level

Paid time off costs at department level

Patient accounts receivable

Patient care hours

Patient complaint rate

Patient satisfaction

Patient wait times, by process step

Patient/staff ratios

Patients who leave without being seen (by day, by time)

Percentage of capital expenses

Percentage of cash flow to total debt

Percentage of cash flow to total liabilities

Percentage of charitable revenue

Percentage of debt to capitalization

Percentage of fixed asset financing

Percentage of in-patient capitated revenue

Percentage of in-patient commercial revenue

Percentage of in-patient HMO revenue

Percentage of in-patient revenue

Percentage of in-patient self-pay revenue

Percentage of Medicaid revenue

Percentage of operating margin

Percentage of outpatient Medicare revenue

Percentage of outpatient revenue

Percentage of part-time FTEs of total FTEs

Percentage of voluntary staff turnover

Physician FTE

Physician productivity (relative value units)

Purchase order (PO) quantity ordered by department

Property, plant, and equipment

Readmission rates

Replacement viability

Reported income index

Reserve levels

Return on equity

Return to vendor

Revenue by contract type

Revenue per physician FTE

Risk-adjusted mortality

Salaries and benefits

Satisfaction with physical examination

Satisfaction with physician

Service line utilization and trends by payer type

Service provision

Short-term investments

Skill levels

Source of hires versus cost

Staff turnover

Staff turnover by job code

Staff turnover by location

Staffing cost trend

Staffing-related quality indicators

Supplies and services

Surgical cases in-patient

Surgical cases out-patient

Times interest earned

Total admissions

Total cash and investments

Total compensation per FTE

Total discharge

Total income

Total liabilities

Total margin

Total operating expenses

Total paid time off of FTEs

Total PO dollar amount

Total revenue per FTE

Total salary per FTE

Total travel distance

Total turnover per manager

Total turnover per tenure

Total unrestricted funds

Turnover of clinical and non-clinical staff

Uncompensated care

Unit efficiency

Unrealized gains

Vacancy rate

Weekly payroll

Working capital absorption

Working capital for current accounting period

Information

Annual cost per reading

Average cost per article

Average cost per subscription

Average dollars per e-mail sent or delivered

Average order size

Average quarter-hour audience

Average revenue per subscription

Average time spent listening per user (day/week/month/year)

Bounce rate

Click to open rate (number of unique clicks/number of unique opens)

Click-through rate

Click-through rate (CTR)

Conversion rate

Conversion rate (number of actions/unique click-throughs)

Conversion rates

Cost per broadcast hour

Cost per consumed (by viewers/listeners) hour

Cost per customer

Cost per lead, prospect, or referral

Cost per production hour

Cost per viewer/listener

Cost per visitor

Cost per action (CPA)

Cumulative audience sessions

Delivery rate (e-mails sent—bounces)

Gross ratings points

Life cycle cost per reading

Local content as a percentage of all content

Net subscribers (number of subscribers plus new subscribers) - (bounces + unsubscribes)

Number of broadcast hours per day/week/month/year

Number of or percentage of spam complaints

Number of orders, transactions, downloads, or actions

Open rate

Output per employee (unique first-run broadcast hours by employee for each medium)

Pay per click (PPC)

Pay per lead (PPL)

Pay per sale (PPS)

Percentage of broadcast hours by genre (news/sports/entertainment, etc.)

Percentage of overhead (non-direct operating costs) against total expenditure

Percentage of orders, transactions, downloads, or actions of e-mails sent or delivered

Percentage unique clicks on a specific recurring link(s)

Referral rate ("send-to-a-friend")

Site stickiness (number of pages visited per visit)

Subscriber retention (number of subscribers—bounces—unsubscribes/ number of subscribers)

Total cost per subscription

Total listener hours (day/week/month/year)

Total revenue

Total revenue per subscription

Unique visitors (total number of unique visitors per day/week/month)

Unsubscribe rate

Utilization of production resources

Value per visitor

Viewers/listeners for each medium as a percentage of total population

Website actions (number of visits to a specific Web page or pages)

Website traffic (total page impressions per day/week/month)

Management of Companies and Enterprises

Capital ratio

Cash position by currency

Cash-to-assets ratio

Cash-to-liabilities ratio

Cash-to–working capital ratio

Cash utilization

Change in residual risk levels

Comparative revenues across offices/subsidiaries/departments

Consolidated payments

Consolidated profits

Consolidated receivables

Consolidated revenues

Consolidated settlements

Cost of equity

Cost to hire management talent

Cost-to-income ratio: By business

Cost-to-income ratio: Consolidated

Days in accounts payable

Days in accounts receivable

Earnings per share

Economic profit

Effectiveness of the risk management practices that are controlling
   material risks

Employee engagement (as measured through survey participation)

Employee movement (such as time in position, transfers, and promotions)

External funds under management

Holding company cash flow

Internal rate of return on new business

Information technology (IT) spending per employee

Level of inherent risk

Long-term debt

Net profit growth

New business profit

Operating profit on long-term investments

Profit diversification

Return on equity

Revenue mix

Short-term debt

Time to hire management talent

Total cash deposits

Manufacturing

Asset utilization

Availability

Avoided cost

Capacity utilization

Comparative analytics for products, plants, divisions, companies

Compliance rates (for government regulations, etc.)

Customer complaints

Customer satisfaction

Cycle time

Demand forecasting

Faults detected prior to failure

First aid visits

First time through

Forecasts of production quantities, etc.

Increase/decrease in plant downtime

Industry benchmark performance

Integration capabilities

Interaction level

Inventory

Job, product costing

Labor as a percentage of cost

Labor usage, costs—direct and indirect

Machine modules reuse

Maintenance cost per unit

Manufacturing cost per unit

Material costing, usage

Mean time between failure (MTBF)

Mean time to repair

Number of production assignments completed in time

On-time orders

On-time shipping

Open orders

Overall equipment effectiveness

Overall production efficiency of a department, plant, or division

Overtime as a percentage of total hours

Percentage decrease in inventory carrying costs

Percentage decrease in production-to-market lead time

Percentage decrease in scrap and rework costs

Percentage decrease in standard production hours

Percentage increase in productivity

Percentage increase in revenues

Percentage material cost reduction

Percentage reduction in defect rates

Percentage reduction in downtime

Percentage reduction in inventory levels

Percentage reduction in manufacturing lead times

Percentage savings in costs

Percentage savings in inventory costs

Percentage savings in labor costs

Percentage savings in transportation costs

Planned work to total work ratio

Predictive maintenance monitoring (maintenance events per cycle)

Process capability

Productivity

Quality improvement (first-pass yield)

Quality tracking—six sigma

Reduced time to productivity

Reduction in penalties

Savings in inventory carrying costs

Scheduled production

Spend analytics

Storehouse stock effectiveness

Supplier trending

Time from order to shipment

Time on floor to be packed

Unplanned capacity expenditure

Unused capacity expenditures

Utilization

Waste ration reduction

Work-in-process (WIP)

Mining

Average bucket weight

Average fuel use per machine

Average loading time

Average number of dumps per hour/day/week/month

Average number of loads per hour/day/week/month

Average payload

Average swing time

Cash operating costs per barrel of oil equivalent (BOE)

Change time (time between cycles)

Cycle distance

Cycle time

Degree of purity and physical characteristics

Dilution of ore

Dump time

Efficiency of metallurgical recovery

Empty stop time

Empty travel distance

Empty travel time

Exploration costs

Finding and development costs

Flitch

Fuel (e.g., gallons/hour)

Gross refining margin

Incident rate (accidents, etc.) per x hours

Lifting costs

Loaded stop time

Loaded travel distance

Loaded travel time

Loading time

Lost time incident frequency rate

Number of equipment failures per day/week/month/year)

Number of holes drilled per day/week/month/year

Oil reserves

Payload

Payload correction (difference between raw and corrected payload)

Percent (metal, etc.) in ore

Percentage uptime (of equipment, plant, etc.)

Product into shed

Production cost per barrel

Production rate—bank cubic meter (BCM)/hour (cubic meters of material moved per hour)

Raw material substitution rate (percentage)

Raw payload

Reserve and resource replacement (percentage)

Tons of ore feed

Tons per hour

Tons per load

Total minutes lost per shift due to breaks

Unit variable costs

Utilization

Waste per ton

Waste recycling (e.g., tons per time unit)

Waste volume

Other Services (Except Public Administration)

Average employee utilization

Average equipment utilization

Average number of days required to repair the item

Average number of no-shows per week/month

Average number of training hours per employee

Average repair cost

Average repair time

Average revenue per service delivered

Cash collected

Collections

Average training cost per employee

Client retention rate

Customer turnover rate

Daily goals

Employee turnover rate

Gross profit on parts/material sold

Idle time

Material cost per service hour sold

Mean service request completion time

Time to close distribution (by time buckets)

Net profit as a percentage of labor sold

Number of apprentices and organized members certified

Number of apprentices and organized members to meet requirements

Number of open service requests

Number of prospective clients converted to clients

Number of service requests resolved during the period

Number of training courses conducted per month/quarter/year

Service level details

Percentage of members participating in approved programs

Percentage of total members participating in meetings

Period service renewal rate

Period service renewals booked value/period service renewals value

Period service renewals value

Repair order mean time to repair

Repair order past due percentage

Sales per employee

Sales per estimator

Sales per production square foot

Sales per production technician

Service booked to renewal ratio

Service contracts activated new business value

Service contracts activated renewals value

Service contracts expired value

Service contracts terminated billed value

Service contracts terminated remaining value

Service department throughput (per day/week/month)

Service level

Service renewal past due percentage

Service renewals booked value

Service renewals forecast

Service renewals uplift

Service request backlog

Service request closed activity

Service request escalated backlog percentage

Service request reopened activity

Service request unassigned backlog percentage

Target membership growth

Total parts/material cost as a percentage of total sales

Unresolved escalated backlog percentage

Unresolved service request backlog

Unresolved unassigned backlog percentage

Weekly team targets

Professional, Scientific, and Technical Services

Annual billable utilization percentage

Availability

Availability (excluding planned downtime)

Average percentage of CPU utilization

Average percentage of memory utilization

Average hourly fee

Average number of virtual images per administrator

Cost of managing processes

Cost of service delivery

Deviation of planned budget for SLA

Downtime

Mean time to repair (MTTR)

Mean time between failure (MTBF)

Number of defects found over period of time

Number of outstanding actions of last SLA review

Percentage of application development work outsourced

Percentage of bugs found in-house

Percentage of consultants generating revenue

Percentage of consulting hours that generate revenue

Percentage of e-mail spam messages stopped/detected

Percentage of outage due to changes (planned unavailability)

Percentage of outage due to incidents (unplanned unavailability)

Percentage of service requests resolved within an agreed-on period of time

Percentage of systems covered by antivirus/antispyware software

Percentage of systems with latest antivirus/antispyware signatures

Percentage of time lost redeveloping applications as a result of source code loss

Percentage of time sheets in need of correction/validation

Percentage of unit tests covering software code

Percentage of user requested features

Profit per project

Quality assurance personnel as percentage of the number of application developers

Software development quality

System usability scale

Time ratio for design to development work

Time-to-market of changes to existing products/services

Total service delivery penalties paid

Unit costs of IT services

Workforce turnover rate

Public Administration

Economic Development

Amount of new retail square footage

Average number of business days before reported graffiti is removed

Cost per animal sterilized

Cost per person trained in workforce development

Cost per sheltered animal

Cost per youth placed in summer youth employment jobs

Development of county-wide infrastructure, land supply, and affordable housing plan within one year, plan implementation and schedule adherence thereafter

Dropout rate of high school students

Health and human services

Housing affordability index/percentage of households that can afford a median-priced home

Net loss of agricultural or environmentally sensitive areas

Number of affordable mortgages financed for eligible low and moderate income families

Number of child care facilities in areas of need

Number of child care facilities with national accreditation

Number of economic development inquiries received

Number of emerging technology projects

Number of existing and start-up businesses and agencies trained by the city or county per year that remain in business after two years

Number of jobs created in the community from economic and community development projects

Number of loans to low and moderate income persons closed per year

Number of low-income infants, toddlers, and preschoolers participating in early childhood development services (versus waiting list)

Number of new assisted living units in public housing within two years

Number of new businesses related to incentives/coordinated efforts to promote growth in targeted industries

Number of new incubated businesses that survive at least two years

Number of special projects completed

Number of successful placements of training program participants in employment within three years

Number of volunteer hours

Number of youth participating in after-school/gap-time programming

Number of youths participating in employment and entrepreneurship programs within two years

Per capita income

Percentage annual increase in new dollars generated for economic development programs

Percentage increase in graduation rate

Percentage of businesses trained and subsequently receiving funding within two years

Percentage of children with insurance

Percentage of people with disabilities satisfied or very satisfied with service access within three years

Percentage of residents satisfied with community involvement process with economic development

Percentage of residents with increased access to primary and specialty medical care

Percentage of sheltered animals adopted

Percentage of youth with improved academic performance

Percentage increase in the number of affordable and special needs housing

Percentage of businesses satisfied or very satisfied with the city/county's business processes

Percentage of customers of the health and human services area satisfied or very satisfied with service delivery and customer care

Percentage of participants who report they learned something that will help them start a business

Percentage of survey respondents earning less than $25,000 per year that rate the city/county's health and human services as good or very good

Percentage of survey respondents that agree the city or county government effectively develops low-income/poor areas

Percentage of users of health and human services satisfied or very satisfied with transit access to health care

Reduced percentage rate of uninsured in the city/county

Sick leave hours used per 1,000 hours

Total infant mortality rate per 1,000 live births

Total mortality rate (all causes) per 100,000

Unemployment rate

Neighborhood and Unincorporated Area Municipal Services

Cost per document released

Net loss of agricultural designated lands outside the urban development boundary (UDB) or environmentally sensitive lands

Number of infill development and infill housing units and infill redevelopment projects per year (completed)

Number of renters assisted

Percentage of lease payments that will be on time

Percentage of tree canopy increase

Percentage of general/nuisance complaints responded to within 48 hours

Percentage of nuisance incidents remediated within predefined timeframes

Percentage of residents and businesses aware of critical knowledge factors of code compliance

Percentage of residents satisfied with information delivery systems

Percentage of roadways and rights-of-way cleaned and well maintained

Percentage of survey respondents that agree the city or county employees that helped them went the extra mile to get their issue heard and resolved

Percentage of survey respondents that rate flooding as a minor or major problem in their neighborhood

Percentage of survey respondents that rate the development and land use/zoning in their neighborhood as good or very good

Percentage of survey respondents that rate the drinking water quality and sewer service as good or very good

Percentage of survey respondents that rate the quality of roadways and road signs in city or county as good or very good

Percentage of survey respondents that were satisfied with their last contact with city or county personnel

Secret shopper rating for employee customer service

Total square feet of facilities

Public Safety

Average fire rescue response time from time dispatch receives life-threatening call from 911 and/or percentage of total fire calls with a response time under eight minutes from call entry to arrival and/or emergency services average response time from public safety answering point (PSAP) to arrival

Cost per park safety enforcement action on park land

Development and implementation of a comprehensive plan for homeland security

Development of a comprehensive plan for homeland security

Increase in number of licensed pets over next three years

Increase number of public emergency shelters by 10% in three years

Number of abandoned vehicles investigated

Number of collisions related to pursuits

Number of first responders trained and equipped for an emergency event

Number of patrol hours in neighborhoods

Number of pedestrian/bicycle collisions per 100,000 population

Number of requests for special operations support

Number of service call responses annually

Percentage increase in number of volunteers over the next three years

Percentage increase in use of non-lethal technology over next three years

Percentage of citizens that state they feel safe in parks and recreation facilities

Percentage reduction in drug-related incidents

Percentage reduction in juvenile crime rates

Percentage reduction in non-emergency calls into the 911 system

Percentage of survey respondents who generally find police officers and traffic enforcement officers to be friendly and approachable safety services

Percentage of survey respondents that rate crime in their neighborhood as a minor or major problem

Percentage reduction in property loss rate

Police emergency average response time (minutes)

Rate of reinstitutionalization of offenders processed through the Juvenile Evaluation Center

Rate of traffic fatalities per 100,000 population

Recreation and Culture

Average cost per daily servicing acre

Average safety rating for pools

Cost per estimated arts center services participant hour

Cost per estimated museum participant hour

Cost per participant hour in senior services

Cost per public event

Increase in the number of collaborative programs and participants with educational institutions

Number of acres of natural areas restored and number of acres maintained

Number of adult sports teams

Number of attendees at recreational, cultural, and library facilities, programs and services

Number of cultural, recreational, and libraries collaboration projects per year

Number of cultural, recreational, and library programs available for the elderly and people with disabilities

Number of developed park acreage

Number of estimated arts center services participant hours

Number of estimated participant hours in after-school programs

Number of meals served to seniors

Number of public art contracts completed

Number of residents satisfied or very satisfied with availability of open or green spaces

Number of residents satisfied or very satisfied with availability of facilities within five years

Park acres per capita

Percentage of free programs offered

Percentage of library district residents within four miles (or 25 minutes) of a library

Percentage of organizations and artists satisfied or very satisfied with the city or county grant application process

Percentage of participants satisfied or very satisfied with availability of quality life-long learning programs in three years

Percentage of survey respondents that rate the city or county's library services as good or very good

Percentage of survey respondents that rate the city or county's recreational and cultural activities as good or very good

Quality rating of residents and visitors for cultural, recreational, and library facilities and places

Recreation and culture dollars available through all sources of funding, including existing and new sources

Resident ratings of the appearance of recreational, cultural, and library facilities

Resident ratings of the range of parks and recreation activities

Total audience served through public events

Transportation

Achievement of all major milestones timelines in the city or county's transportation plan

Annual percentage change of parking operations expense

Average commute times to work in minutes

Average dollar value per central purchasing office purchase order

Average number of days between invoice date and date of check disbursement

Bond ratings

Calendar days from requisition to purchase order

Cost of government: Dollars per capita and per capita by category

Daily bus and rail boardings

Dollar amount of purchases made that meet sustainability guidelines

Dollar cost per accounts payable transaction

Enabling strategies: Budgets and finance

Implementation of 24-hour rail and bus operations

Improved national customer satisfaction ranking for the airport to one of the top 20–ranked airports within two years

Increase average work-trip vehicle occupancy from an estimated 1.1 passengers per vehicle to 1.15 passengers per vehicle

Increase in compliance with local tax collection by 5% over next five years

Increase in percentage of public transit trips taken

Increase in number of visitors to county transit websites

Increase the customer satisfaction ranking for the seaport by 1.5 percent by year xxxx

National customer satisfaction ranking the airport among the top-ten airports for passenger satisfaction by year xxxx

Negotiated contract savings (dollars saved)

Net parking income/loss

Number (and percentage) of facilities meeting regulatory requirements

Number of audits and special projects completed

Number of parking tickets issued

Number of payment transactions processed for departments

Number of projects managed

Number of purchases made city/countywide by central purchasing office

Number of residents satisfied or very satisfied with the implementation of the city/county's transportation plan

Percentage of audit recommendations "concurred with" by management

Percentage of cash reserves

Percentage of strategic plans outcomes supported by business plans

Percentage of traffic signals synchronized and optimized

Percentage of vendor solicitations successfully awarded without delay due to re-bids or protests

Percentage of community satisfied with value of city or county's services for tax dollars paid

Percentage of employees rating the city or county or state as a good place to work

Percentage of internal users satisfied with procurement timeliness quality, and overall service

Percentage of survey respondents that rate the cleanliness of buses and train cars as good or very good

Percentage of survey respondents that rate the congestion on the roadways in their neighborhood as a minor or major problem

Percentage of survey respondents that rate the convenience of the city or county bus routes as good or very good

Percentage of survey respondents that rate the ease of transportation to and from the airport and seaport as good or very good

Planned frequency of transit service during peak and non-peak hours

Rate of schedule adherence for bus and rail service

Receiving Government Finance Officers Association (GFOA) distinguished budget award

Total number of aviation passengers

Enabling Strategies: Government Operations

Cost per page view on the city or county website

Dollars saved through IT investments

Electronic access to services and information, and percentage of survey respondents that agree that it is easy to find what they need or want on the city or county website

Fleet costs (acquisition, operating, resale value) within prescribed industry standards and percentage of department users satisfied with quality and timeliness of fleet management services

Increase number of employees rating the city or county as a good place to work

Number of page views on the city or county website per capita

Number of planned media events (includes news conferences)

One hundred percent of financial reports filed timely and accurately in compliance with the law

Percentage of city or county employees aware of their component of performance targets

Percentage of city or county employees aware of their importance to city or county's values and priorities

Percentage of IT projects completed on time, within budget

Percentage of IT routine problems solved within 24 hours

Percentage of (facility) projects completed within budget and on time

Percentage of accuracy between votes cast and votes reported

Percentage of customers familiar with city or county sources of information

Percentage of internal customers and residents satisfied with aesthetics of city or county facilities

Percentage of residents with a positive image of city or county government

Percentage of users (residents, visitors, employees, etc.) satisfied with city or county services

Reduced staff turnover

Satisfaction ratings from service delivery departments

Value of corporate-initiated media coverage

Voter satisfaction with process

Real Estate and Rental and Leasing

Realtor Website

Conversation rate (i.e., take rate): Number of conversations over number of website visits

Top conversion page exit: The page where website visitors change their minds and exit your website.

Traffic source percentage: Website visits referred by

Real Estate Office

Advertising and promotion

Average commission per sale

Average commission per salesperson

Commission margin

Net profit

Office cost (telephone, fax, and other office cost)

Rent cost of premises

Sold homes per available inventory ratio

Total income

Wages and salaries (including commissions and vehicle allowances)

Year-to-year variance on average sold price

Year-to-year variance on dollar volume of sold listings

Year-to-year variance on sold average dollar per square foot

Commercial Property Management

Annual return on investment in percentage

Construction/purchaser rate: New constructed or purchased units over time

Cost per square foot

Equity value growth in percentage

Lease events coverage ratio: Number of lease inquiries over number of available units

Management efficiency: Number of leased spaces over number of staff

Market share growth

Monthly return on investment as percentage

Occupancy cost: Cost per occupied unit

Operation cost-to–rent income ratio

Percentage of rent collected

Price to income as percentage

Profitability per square foot

Real estate demand growth: Market rental demands

Rented space usage quality: Average number of tenant visits over rented space

Renting cost: Renting cost per square foot

Renting return on investment: Rent income over cost

Revenue per square foot

Risk metrics as percentage

Total property management income per property manager

Usage efficiency: Available renting square feet over number of staff

Utilization (vacancy) rate: Rented square feet over total square feet, or rented units over total units

Real Estate Investor

Average gross multiplier for portfolio

Cost-per-square-foot–to–value-per-square-foot ratio

Equity-to-value ratio

Gross multiplier per commercial property

LTV (loan-to-value) ratio per property

Mortgage rate index

Overall LTV (loan-to-value) ratio for portfolio

Price-per-square-foot–to–value-per-square-foot ratio

Profitability per square foot

Property value growth (market trend)

Purchase price–to–appraisal value ratio

Rental value growth rate

ROI (return on investment)

Retail Trade

Product Sales

Cost of goods sold

Gross profit budget percentage

Sales budget percentage

Discount

Gross profit

Gross profit and prognostics

Gross profit and prognostics percentage

Gross profit budget

Gross profit campaign

Gross profit percentage KPI

Gross profit prognostics

Gross profit prognostics percentage

Gross profit standard

Gross profit year-to-date

Number of stores

Product quantity

Average inventory

Sales

Sales and prognostics

Sales campaign

Sales growth period

Sales growth year

Sales growth year by week

Sales prognostics

Sales standard

Sales trend percentage KPI

Sales value-added tax (VAT)

Sales view

Sales view year-to-date

Share prognostics

Time range

Total number of stores

Finance and Accounting

Accounts payable turnover

Accounts receivable turnover days

Acid test ratio

Administrative cost percentage

Break-even (dollars)

Cash conversion cycle

Contribution margin

Cost of goods

Cost of goods sold

Current ratio

Ending inventory at retail

Gross margin

Gross margin return on investment

Initial mark-up

Interest cost percentage

Inventory turnover

Maintained mark-up (dollars)

Margin percentage

Mark-up percentage

Net receipts

Net sales

Retail price

Return on capital invested

Sales per square foot

Stock turnover days

Total asset sales ratio

Turnover

Salary

Real absence hours

Real absence share

Real GPWH

Real overtime hours

Real overtime share

Real TWH

Real working hours

Salary

Salary amount

Salary amount exchange currency

Salary hours

Salary turnover share

Salary Targets

Real absence hours

Real GP work hours

Real total work hours

Salary absence percentage

Salary GP work hour

Salary overtime percentage

Salary target absence percentage

Salary target GP work hour

Salary target overtime percentage

Salary target turnover percentage

Salary target work hour

Salary turnover percentage

Hourly Sales

Customers per hour

Discount

Gross profit

Items

Margin per customer

Number of customers

Sales growth year

Sales growth year percentage

Sales last year

Sales per customer

Sales trend percentage

Sales view

Total number of stores

Budget Sales

Budget gross profit

Budget number of customers

Budget sales

Customers

Discount

Gross profit

Items

Sales

Sales exchange currency

Sales VAT

Payment with Point-of-Sale (POS) Statistics

Amount

Amount exchange currency

Items

Number of customers

Number of items

Refund amount

Refund count

Sales income VAT

Time range

Transaction cancel amount

Transaction cancel count

Transaction cancel percentage

Void amount

Void count

Void percentage

Zero sale count

Hourly Product Sales

Gross profit percentage

Item discount

Item gross profit

Item quantity

Item sales

Item sales exchange currency

Item sales VAT

Items sold

Transportation and Warehousing

Annualized inventory turns

Annualized cost of goods sold (COGS)/average daily inventory value

Backlog value

Value of open, not yet fulfilled, booked order lines

Book-to-fulfill ratio

Booked order value/fulfilled value

Book to ship days

Average of shipped date: Firm date (booked date used if no firmed date)

Booked order value

Booked order line value (not including returns)

Claims percentage for freight costs

Customer order promised cycle time

Defects per million opportunities

Inventory months of supply

On-time line count

On-time pickups

Pick exceptions rate

Percentage of picks with exceptions

Pick release to ship

Planned inventory turns

Planned cost of goods sold/planned inventory value

Planned margin

Planned revenue: Planned costs

Planned margin percentage

Planned margin/planned revenue

Planned on-time shipment

Planned service level (percentage of shipments shipped on time)

Planned resource utilization

Planned resource usage

Product revenue

Product sales revenue (not including service) recognized in selected period (based on AR invoice lines)

Product revenue backlog

Value of booked order lines less returns plus deferred revenue backlog (invoiced but not recognized)

Production value

Value of work-in-process (WIP) completions into inventory

Production to plan rate

Production standard value/planned standard value

Receipt to put-away

Time elapsed from pick release to ship confirm

Time elapsed from receipt

Transit time

Utilities

Annual labor cost per device

Average cost per job category

Average cost per megawatt produced

Average labor hours per device per year

Average maintenance cost per mile of pipe/line/cable

Average number of days each work order is past due

Average number of labor hours to complete a maintenance task

Average response time to fix breaks

Average revenue per megawatt produced

Average time to settle a rate case

Consumption analyzed by units consumed and target reduction achieved

Crew productivity

Drinking water quality: Percentage of water tests that meet regulatory standards

Electrical grid load

Equipment failure rate

Equipment unavailability, hours per year: Planned maintenance

Equipment unavailability, hours per year: Sustained fault

Equipment unavailability, hours per year: Temporary fault

Equipment unavailability, hours per year: Unplanned maintenance

Maintenance backlog

Maintenance cost as a percentage of manufacturing cost

Maintenance technician's skill level improvement, year over-year

Mean time to repair

Number of complaints received by type

Number of customers who were cut off due to violations of regulations

Number of disconnections

Number of pending work orders

Number of power failures per year

Number of reported gas leakages per 1,000 households

Number of sewage blockages per month/year

Number of staff per 1,000 customer connections

Number of uncontrolled sewage overflows affecting private properties

Outage time per event

Percentage of customers that would characterize their bills as accurate and timely

Percentage of possible power revenue billed

Percentage reduction in number of complaints to the local regulatory body

Percentage reduction in number of employee injuries

Percentage reduction in number of equipment failures

Percentage of maintenance work orders requiring rework

Percentage of man-hours used for proactive work

Percentage of scheduled man-hours to total man-hours

Profit redistribution (rural electric coops)

Reduction in hazardous liquid spill notification time

Reduction or stabilization in rates (municipally owned utilities)

Response time to gas or water leaks

Sewage system reliability

Station unavailability: Planned maintenance

Station unavailability: Sustained fault

Station unavailability: Temporary fault

Total shareholder returns (investor-owned utilities)

Total time to complete new customer connections

Transformer/pump station reliability

Voltage deviations per year

Water system reliability

Wholesale Trade

Dock turnaround time

Freight costs (minimize costs without affecting deliveries)

Inventory accuracy, stockouts

Inventory carrying costs

Inventory turns per year

Logistics costs per year

Low-velocity inventory comparison through sectors

Order fill rate and accuracy

Technology used to execute inventory strategies

Warehouse flow-through (or some measure of yard or warehouse productivity)

Wholesale revenue

Total factor productivity

Labor productivity

Return on assets

Profit margin

Debt to equity

Inventory turnover

Asset utilization

Collection efficiency

About the Authors

Nils Rasmussen, BA, MBA, is the CEO at Solver, Inc., an international company that provides implementation of comprehensive performance management, planning, analytics, scorecard, and dashboard solutions. He is the coauthor of three titles published by John Wiley & Sons.

Claire Y. Chen is the Chief Business Intelligence Architect at Solver, Inc., and the Microsoft Virtual Technology Specialist in the Southern California region. She is well experienced in providing data warehouse and business intelligence solutions via multiple technologies in various industries.

Manish Bansal, BE, MS, is the Vice President at Solver, Inc., and advises companies on various ways to improve performance by leveraging technology solutions. He is an experienced management consultant who has worked across various industries and functional areas, with a special focus to deliver value.

Index